THE
INTERPRETATION
OF
Dreams
IN
CHINESE
CULTURE

Hou Xiang Sheng, a master of medicine and alchemy, in the guise of a frog (Wang).

THE
INTERPRETATION
OF
Dreams
IN
CHINESE
CULTURE

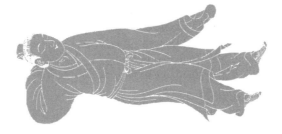

BY

FANG JING PEI

&

ZHANG JUWEN

WEATHERHILL

In the captions to the woodblock illustrations (Wang) refers to the *Lie Xian Quan Zhuan (Complete Biographies of the Immortals)*, compiled by Wang Shizhen in 1601; (Jin) refers to *Wu Shuang Pu (Unprecedented Biographies)* by Jin Guliang, published 1690–1699; and (Xiao) refers to the Qing-dynasty edition of Xiao Yuncong's *Illustrations to the Li Sao*.

First edition, 2000

Published by Weatherhill, Inc., 41 Monroe Turnpike, Trumbull, CT 06611. Protected by copyright under the terms of the International Copyright Union; all rights reserved. Except for fair use in book reviews, no part of this book may be reproduced for any reason by any means, including any method of photographic reproduction, without permission of Weatherhill, Inc. Printed in the United States.

05 04 03 02 01 10 9 8 7 6 5 4 3 2 1

Library of Congress Cataloging-in-Publication Data

Fang, Jing Pei.
    The interpretation of dreams in Chinese culture / by Fang Jing Pei &
    Zhang Juwen
            p. cm.
    Includes bibliographic references.
    ISBN 0-8348-0437-9
        1. Dreams--China. 2. Dream interpretation--China. 3. Dreams in literature.
    4. China--Civilization. I. Zhang, Juwen. II. Title

BF1098.C5 F36 2000
154.6'3'0951--dc21   00-035205

CONTENTS

ACKNOWLEDGMENTS
6

CHRONOLOGY OF CHINESE HISTORY
7

INTRODUCTION
9

PART ONE
Theories and Dream Interpreters
19

PART TWO
Dream Symbols and Their Interpretations
45

SOURCES AND BIBLIOGRAPHY
155

ACKNOWLEDGMENTS

The two authors of this work, one born in China and one in the United States, represent through their different backgrounds two different perspectives on the culture of their ancestry. Working in collaboration, each has opened a door to the other's world and been enriched through the experience. Researching and putting this work to paper has been rewarding from many aspects, and the many people who have provided information, comments, encouragement, and suggestions have also enhanced the collaborative effort. Among them are Toni and Ed Shapiro, Priscilla and Robert Foley, Dr. Susan Blader, Beverly Boucher, Yan Liu, Chang Jiang, and Wang Su Yan. To Jing Liu and Dr. Colin Johnstone we are most grateful for your tireless support.

A Chronology of Chinese History

Xia dynasty	ca. 2100 – ca. 1600 B.C.
Shang dynasty	ca. 1600 – ca. 1100 B.C.
Western Zhou dynasty	ca. 1100 – 771 B.C.
Eastern Zhou dynasty	ca. 770 – 256 B.C.
Spring and Autumn period	770 – 476 B.C.
Warring States period	475 – 221 B.C.
Qin dynasty	221 – 206 B.C.
Western Han dynasty	206 B.C. – 24 A.D.
Eastern Han dynasty	25 – 220 A.D.
Three Kingdoms period	220 – 265
Western Jin dynasty	265 – 316
Eastern Jin dynasty	317 – 420
Southern Dynasties	317 – 589
Northern Dynasties	386 – 581
Sui dynasty	581 – 618
Tang dynasty	618 – 907
Five Dynasties (north)	907 – 960
Ten Kingdoms (south)	907 – 979
Liao dynasty	907 – 1125
Northern Song dynasty	907 – 1127
Southern Song dynasty	1127 – 1279
Jin dynasty	1115 – 1234
Yuan dynasty	1271 – 1368
Ming dynasty	1368 – 1644
Qing dynasty	1644 – 1911
Republic of China	1912 – 1949
People's Republic of China	1949 –

莊伯微

Zhuang Bo became a Daoist master by daydreaming for thirty years (Wang).

INTRODUCTION

Do dreams hold special messages? Do dreams predict future events? Do dreams hold clues to underlying conflicts? Do dreams serve as outlets allowing fears and desires to be expressed in an acceptable form? Or do dreams lack all rational meaning, but merely reflect the brain's electrical and chemical mechanisms at work?

People have long been fascinated with dreams and their meanings. Myriad books and articles have been written on these subjects in every language and culture, arguably the most famous being Freud's text on the interpretation of dreams. One proposal certainly true is that dream interpretation must be provided within the context of the dreamer's culture. Culture provides the framework of basic meanings for one's life experience. It provides the understanding of what is accepted and what is not, what is good and what is bad, the meanings of symbols, the definitions of good and evil, goals and objectives, and so on.

For example, the birth of a female child in the West is a joyous event, greeted no differently than the the birth of a male child. Yet in China and other countries, the birth of a female child has traditionally been viewed negatively. To ensure survival of the family, and to maintain agricultural productivity, male offspring were preferred. Any omens seen as indicators of the sex of a child soon to be born can therefore only be interpreted in the context of that culture's attitudes toward male and female children. Without understanding the norms of the culture, we cannot interpret specific dream imagery; conversely, however, we can say that understanding how dreams are interpreted can provide insight into another culture.

The purpose of this book is to provide readers with the Chinese interpretation of the most common dream symbols and their historical references in Chinese literature. The diversity of Chinese culture is so great that any generalization of a particular interpretation provides somewhat of a distorted image. However, if it is necessary to understand dream interpretation within the context of its cultural, social, and historical foundation, each individual dream interpretation is an aid to establishing this larger frame of reference. Of course, each of the various ethnic groups that make up the China of today had its own folk stories and beliefs, which through centuries of wars and conquests have been assimilated into dream interpretations of the nation as a whole and become a part of contemporary life. This book attempts to present those interpretations in their historical context, rather than reinterpret them based on today's understanding.

Following is a brief outline of the place of dream interpretation in Chinese folk culture, as well as its various methods, in turn followed by a brief review of the history of dream interpretation. Basic information is drawn from Chinese literature spanning more than two thousand years, including collections of Chinese folk tales, religious and philosophical texts, dynastic histories, and imperial compilations. The woodblock illustrations, taken from some of those texts, are by well-known artists of the Ming dynasty. They depict many figures from folk tales and legends, providing a visual aid to understanding the stories presented.

Cultural Role of Dream Interpretation

Dream interpretation plays an important role in Chinese culture, particularly in folk culture. Because of the diversity and size of China, its culture consists of many individualized cultures, including the formal culture of its ruling elite as well as specific ethnic and regional cultures. If culture is composed of not only the great inventions, classic texts, and magnificent structures, but includes the world view of the common person, then dream interpretations and stories on which the interpretations are based can provide an excellent tool with which to analyze and understand culture.

The cultural and social changes in China, especially in the past century and a half, have been immeasurable, and one may assume that the meanings of the dream symbols have changed concurrently. Yet while the forms and manner of expression change along with societal changes, the core meanings of these symbols remain relative stable. If we look at China's cultural core, formed by its philosophical values and virtues, we find changes which are less dramatic in comparison to the changes at the outer layers of its cultural identity, such as ways of dressing, eating, and speaking. Traditions rely upon core beliefs and values as opposed to trends, the influences of the moment. The stability of traditions that have remained constant for generations cannot easily be changed by law or edict. One need only look at contemporary China to see manifestations of traditional folkways that were supposedly legislated out of existence. Changes in tradition occur only over long periods of time, most commonly when there is an infusion of beliefs from another culture that through the passage of time become amalgamated with the original culture.

In fact, while the cultural values reflected in dream interpretation appear today similar to any period in Chinese history, we sometimes find the symbols themselves are altered to carry a traditional meaning effectively. For example, interpretations related to riding horses have been transferred to automobiles, the current mode of transportation. And, while Chinese today may seek dream interpreters less often than in the past, actions still are strongly influenced by traditional interpretations.

Interpreting dreams played an important role in the politics of China from the earliest times. Men in power utilized dream interpretation, both consciously and unconsciously, to maintain the primacy of the state, while the common people utilized dream interpretation to coordinate their relations in smaller groups. As in other tribal societies and feudal empires, rulers imposed their personal will or desires through evoking the messages of dreams or the edicts of gods. In China, ancestral worship further strengthened belief in dreams, since ghosts of ancestors commonly offered instruction or influenced the affairs of living generations. And as elders, they had to be placated and obeyed, since both state and family were based on the Confucian hierarchy of relationships, which demanded that sons obey fathers, wives obey husbands, ministers obey the emperor, etc.

Early in the Shang and Zhou dynasties, tortoise shells were utilized in a sophisticated system of prognostication. The shells were heated and the resulting cracks were interpreted as characters that held interpretations of dreams and questions. It is documented that rulers in the Zhou Dynasty used dream interpretation as a tool in making polices for ruling the empire.

Thus the earliest culture of China was primarily one of divination, and saw the invention of the bone inscriptions and other utensils and wares for that purpose. For example, early in the Shang Dynasty it is recorded that a person named Gu was the most important dream interpreter in the court. In the ensuing Zhou Dynasty, a position called Tai Pu was established in the court for an official in charge of dream interpretation and other forms of divination. In fact, in every dynasty there were dream interpreters at court, involved in the political affairs of the time.

As a normal policy of economic management, for example, it was common for rulers and their scholar-officials to invoke the capricious power of Heaven *(tian)* to ensure good crops and to avoid natural disasters, and to empower themselves by interpreting related dreams and omens. Dreams of "grain" (see entries), for example, usually indicate good luck and harvest, while the negative connotations of "rain" and "water" obviously derived from economic concerns. It was also common to take advantage of natural disasters leading to economic decline as a means to impose political and economic reforms. And, of course, the ruler could impose his personal desires in the name of a dream.

Confucianism, Daoism, and Buddhism, the three main belief systems of China, all developed religious, philosophical, and popular components, which in turn combined with traditional myths and local folk beliefs. Philosophical and religious ideas are therefore integrated and reflected in popular and practical dream interpretations. The classifications of Six Dreams in the pre-Qin period and Ten Dreams by Wang Fu in the Han dynasty are predominantly based on Confucian concepts, but contain Daoist transcendental ideals. The Four Dreams and Five Dreams classification systems were claimed to be Buddhist inspired but are influenced as well by the Daoist understanding of the human body.

The symbols and the meanings of dreams function as a medium to facilitate communications within a group. It is likely that the concepts of "lucky dream" and "disastrous dream" led people to pursue the "dream god," "dream ghost," or "evil-avoiding dream" (see Part One). Through these practices, beliefs are reinforced and developed and new contexts allow new meanings to be attached to new symbols. The process is dynamic.

Dreams or dream metaphors are numerous in the works of scholars, for whom they functioned not only as a vision of a utopian world, where one could avoid the conflicts and pressures of involvement in worldly affairs, but also an indirect means of criticizing the actual status quo. The tradition of the Chinese intelligentsia of expressing their ideals through symbols and metaphors can be seen in poetry, painting, calligraphy, artifacts, and even architecture. For example, the classic literature of *Zhuang Zi* in the Warring States period, *Liao Zhai Zhi Yi (Strange and Ghost Stories)* by Pu Songling, and *Hong Lou Meng (Dreams of the Red Chamber)* by Cao Xueqin in the Qing dynasty use dreams as a medium to express the authors' thoughts about the social realities of their times.

Traditional Chinese medicine is entirely based on the cosmological concepts of five elements, Yin and Yang, and Qi. In the earliest Chinese medical text, *Huang Di Nei Jing (The Yellow Emperor's Book of Internal Medicine)*, human diseases are explained with many references to dreaming. Chen Shi Yuan's theory of Nine Dreams, for example, relies largely upon the medical explanations of the operations of the human organs. It is certainly a culture-bound perspective that an essential system of medicine in one culture is considered to be "alternative" in another.

Arts of Divination and Prognostication

The domain of Chinese folk culture from which dream interpretation or dream divination derives its theories and methods is more broadly referred to as *fangshu*, arts combining *fang* and *shu*. According to *Wen Xin Diao Long (The Literary Heart and the Carving of Dragons)*, the earliest and most important book of literary criticism, *fang* means medicine and *shu* means calculation, calendar, and mathematics. The extensive area of inquiry covered by *fangshu* can be seen from the following list of arts and practices:

pu shi shu: An art of divining by using the stem of an alpine yarrow *(Achillea alpina)* plant, popular before the Qin dynasty and continuing through the Qing dynasty.

zhan xing shu: An art to predict natural and human events by studying the location, shape, distance, and other changes of the celestial bodies. As Western astrology, it is intertwined with the development of astronomy in China.

zhan hou shu: An art of divining the auspicious or ill omens of the future through natural phenomena.

xing ming shu: An art of associating the celestial bodies with human beings to discover an individual's fortune, emphasizing that each person's fate is related to a celestial body.

suan ming shu: An art of telling an individual's fate by the principles of Yin and Yang, five elements, eight characters, etc., based on the assumption that one's fate is decided before birth.

qi men dun jia shu: An art of studying space and time based on the organization of the Ten Heavenly Stems and Twelve Earthly Branches and their relationship to one another.

tai yi shu: Tai Yi is the metaphoric name for Polaris, a star representing the Heavenly Emperor. It is said to move according to the principles of the five elements and Yin and Yang.

liu ren shu: An art of combining Yin and Yang, and five elements with the Heavenly Stems and Earthly Branches.

ze ri shu: An art of choosing lucky dates to ensure successful outcomes of important activities. This has been practiced in various ways throughout recorded Chinese history.

fu ji shu: Also called *fu qi,* a method of prognostication through two people drawing while holding a stick with a pen tied to it, the resulting drawing portending good or ill.

xiang shu: An art of judging one's character, experience, and future according to appearance, related to traditional medical diagnostic methods.

ce zi shu: An art of predicting by reassembling and reorganizing the writing of characters.

zhan meng shu: An art of explaining human dreams.

feng shui shu (also called *kan xing shu):* An art for choosing auspicious locations for both the living and the dead, practiced not only at the folk level, but influencing the design and construction of imperial architecture.

lian dan shu: An art based on: 1) metallurgy as material condition; 2) ghost (soul) belief as mental condition; and 3) Yin and Yang and five elements as a theoretical condition. It is developed into two schools: *nei dan shu* (internal essence refining) and *wai dan shu* (external essence refining), the former also known as *qi gong,* a form of what is known as *gongfu* (kung fu) in the West. The latter is deeply intertwined with the development of Chinese medicine.

fang zhong shu: An art of maintaining sexuality and sexual intercourse between men and women.

zhong yi shu: Chinese medicine, which is essentially based on the principles of Yin and Yang and the five elements, having gradually developed out of magical practices using various other media and principles

wu gu shu: An art used by witches and sorceresses in which poisonous worms in a jar fought one another, with the outcome used to predict the future.

jiang shen shu: An art of communicating with the gods or ghosts, similar to the seance.

huan shu: An art similar to the practice of modern magicians.

While not all *fangshu* are currently practiced, all have been well documented in the historical literature. Some, for example, *tai yi shu, liu ren shu,* and *fu ji shu,* are rarely known today, while *gongfu* (kung fu) and Chinese medicine are intensively studied in the West.

History of Dream Interpretation

The history of dream interpretation is as old as the history of humanity itself, as it is reasonable to assume that human beings began to think about their dreams as soon as they began to dream. In the course of Chinese history, dream interpretation has been utilized as a political tool, as philosophical argumentation, as a source of superstition, as a proof of other-worldly activities, and as a channel to understand the self. Its popularity has at various periods fluctuated, but its important role in the daily lives of ordinary people and in the formation of the Chinese culture is unquestioned.

Dream interpretation established itself as a necessary political and cultural function as a part of divination, at least by the Shang dynasty, when bone inscriptions, or "oracle bones," were widely used in prognostication. In the traditional Chinese literature relating to dreams, there are two types of text: 1) collections of dreams and dream interpretations to promote certain beliefs for political, cultural, or economic purposes; and 2) compilations of counter-examples that criticize the former. In terms of its concepts and methods, the interpretation of dreams has experienced three transitions: 1) from official to unofficial; 2) from one religious or philosophical approach to multiple religious or philosophical approaches, or from monotheism to polytheism; and 3) from direct interpretation to indirect, symbolic, or even counter-interpretation.

These transitions are felt to be the results of social change and the expansion of knowledge about mankind and nature and their relationship. For example, before the first transition, during the Shang and Zhou dynasties, there were official positions in the imperial courts for those who specialized in dream interpretation and other types of divination. Such an official position gradually disappeared by the Han dynasty and became a role filled by witches or sorceresses. In fact, however, such a change was more in form than in function, as there were always ministers or scholars in the court interpreting dreams for the emperors, as we will see in Part One.

The second transition reflects changes in the Chinese world view from early pantheist and mythological beliefs, which were basically nature-centered, to complex philosophical thinking, which was essentially human-centered. For example, the Shang dynasty bone inscriptions, the earliest extant example of the Chinese written language, were used in divination, sacrifices, or magical rituals. Shang culture was based on the central belief in *tian* (Sky, or Heaven, or Sun-centered universe). However, by the late Zhou period, many new systems of thought had developed, laying the foundation of for polytheist religious systems such as Daoism, and human-oriented ethical codes, such as Confucianism and Legalism. This early and nearly simultaneous flowering of muliple philosophical and religious systems is unique to Chinese culture, and may explain why monotheist European culture is exclusive while the polytheist Chinese culture is inclusive. It is within this eclectic cultural framework that dream interpreters throughout history have developed their various theories and methods, influenced by and oriented toward different religious or philosophical systems, some even contradictory, as will be seen in Part One.

The third transition, from direct interpretation to indirect, symbolic or even counter-interpretation was also the result of the integration of different religious and philosophical sytems over the course of time. Buddhism had the greatest "foreign" impact on Chinese culture, and the key classification systems of of Four Dreams and Five Dreams, formulated during the Tang dynasty, were influenced by Buddhist tenets. Even within the "indigenous" belief systems of Confucianism, Daoism, and others, there appeared contradictory systems such as the Ten Dreams of Wang Fu, a materialist and atheist philosopher of the Han dynasty, and Three Dream classification system, claimed to have been formulated by Confucian thinkers of the late Zhou and early Han dynasties. By the Song and Ming dynasties, the fundamental three doctrines of China—Confucianism, Buddhism, and Daoism—had each established its own system of dream interpretation, and these have co-existed until today.

Viewing the social and historical context of dream interpretation, one observes that the more the society undergoes severe change, the more that dream interpretation or divination is practiced. History shows that times when dream interpreters develop new theories and methods coincide with dynastic falls or periods of great economic or social difficulty. Over the long course of Chinese history, there have been many such periods. For example, during the Spring and Autumn and Warring States periods, the empire was fragmented and developed into many states engaged in endless warfare. This was also the time when the important indigenous Chinese philosophies were established, and *The Book of Change (I Ching, or Yi Jing)* was complet ed and was being widely used. The classification system of Three Dreams was a Confucian system of dream interpretation developed during that period. The fall of the Tang and the end of the Song dynasties are similar periods of intellectual flowering during political upheaval.

It is thus clear that Chinese dream interpretation is a product of social and cultural development and also provides an interpretation of cultural history. Moreover the social and cultural context can never be ignored when discussing Chinese dream interpretation.

Lao Zi, legendary founder of Daoism, riding a water buffalo (Wang).

PART ONE

Theories
and
Dream
Interpreters

*T*he mystery and meaning of dreams were of interest to the earliest Chinese. As have people of all cultures throughout the ages, early Chinese sought to find the connection between these fantastic sleep images and the ordinary reality of daily life. That there was considerable interest in dream images and considerable importance placed on interpreting their meanings is documented in texts from every dynasty since the Zhou. This predilection, which includes a strong interest in myth and folklore, has continued through the modern era. Naturally, the existing documentation records and relates to dreams of the the literati and nobility. However this is simply because the peasant class lacked the tools to record their dreams and their interpretations. Only for those peasants who were able to rise to the literati class do we find references to their dream experiences. But it is the literati and ruling class that set the standards for those beneath them, and it can be surmised that their understanding of dreams and dream interpretations influenced and thus reflects those of the peasant class. This can best be seen in the many commonly shared superstitions and folk beliefs that cut across all classes in every dynasty. The following are some of the most common, traditional schemes for classifying dreams by types, and some of the classic texts in which they are presented.

The Three Dreams (san meng) Classification System

The earliest reference in China to dreams is said to be in *The Rites of Zhou (Zhou Li),* one of the earliest of Chinese books, the title referring to the rituals of rulers of the Zhou dynasty. Although the original text is no longer in existence, versions annotated by Confucian scholars of later periods, from the late Spring and Autumn period through the Han dynasty, contain many references this early work. One can surmise that although these scholars edited the original work, the basic framework of the book is that written in the Zhou period.

The Rites of Zhou indicates that dreams were obviously of importance to the emperor, since matters relating to dream interpretation were assigned to a court official, identified by the title Tai Pu. The Tai Pu was responsible for predicting coming good fortune or disaster, and a major tool for making these predictions was interpreting dreams, primarily those of the emperor and the ruling family, and those who held influential positions. The fact that the Tai Pu held a court position indicates that dreams were utilized not only a matter of personal interest and decision-making but also for setting policies to save and serve the empire. The latter function is illustrated in many documented anecdotes in numerous ancient works on dreams.

Dreams documented in *The Rites of Zhou* were placed in one of three categories:

1) *zhi meng,* those with causes leading one to dream;

2) *ji meng,* various strange dreams or dreams of dreaming; and

3) *xian zhi,* dreams of interaction between the dreamer and spirits.

From the text we know that this Three Dreams classification was correlated to the Three Symptoms in medicine and the Three Changes in metaphysical speculation. However, no further information regarding these three classifications is given, and we do not have enough specific examples to reveal clearly what each of these categories implied. A later compilation presents the Three Dreams classification system as three distinct chapters, and tells us that the original texts may well have been three separate books written in the Xia, Shang, and Zhou dynasties, respectively.

The Four Dreams *(si meng)* Classification System

Buddhism was founded in northern India by Prince Siddhartha around the fifth century B.C. China, after centuries of warfare and division, was finally united in the third century B.C., leading to the relatively peaceful four centuries of the Han dynasty, and it was during the latter part of this dynasty that Buddhism established a foothold there. Buddhism was to have a profound effect, for to the Chinese, long accustomed to conflict, the new religion brought hope and change. It not only brought teachings of nonviolence and peace, it acknowledged that life on earth was fraught with suffering, and perhaps most importantly, it offered the comfort of life after death.

Buddhists also were interested in dreams. *The Legal Garden and Pearl Forest* introduced a classification scheme that divided dreams into one of four types (*si meng,* or Four Dreams):

> 1) *si da bu he meng,* imbalance of the four elements. These dreams usually featured acts or objects of obvious symbolic content, for example, the collapse of mountains, flying through the heavens, being chased by tigers, etc., and were said to reflect an imbalance in the body of the four elements, i.e., earth, water, fire, and wind.

> 2) *xian jian meng,* foreseeing dreams. This dream type identified a connection between dreams and waking experience. If one dreamed of seeing a particular person or thing, one would likely see that person or thing next day or soon thereafter.

> 3) *tian ren meng,* heaven and human dreams. This type of dream was caused by forces emanating from outside of the body, typically the result of extrasensory communication between heaven and humans. In general, good people have good dreams of this type, and thus reinforced the natural goodness in their hearts; bad people, on the other hand, as a consequence of their bad actions have bad dreams. These bad dreams, however, could frighten them and stimulate what goodness existed within them, thereby helping overcoming the evil in their natures. One can infer from this that not every individual was seen to be entirely good or bad but a combination of both, and that there were forces at work to assist in overcoming evil.

4) *xiang meng,* thinking dreams. This type of dream was influenced by the thoughts experienced during the day or while awake. These thinking dreams were, so to speak, the reflections on one's thinking, but done while sleeping.

The Five Dreams *(wu meng)* Classification System

Yet another categorization scheme associated with Buddhism is recorded in the translation of the Buddhist scripture *Pi Po Sha Lun (The Book of Pi Po Sha)* by the well-known traveler-monk of the Tang dynasty, Xuan Zang. In this text, dreams are categorized into five types based on psychological and physiological influences on the individual. The Five Dreams identified were:

1) *yu ta yin meng,* dreams induced by other things;

2) *yu zeng geng meng,* dreams due to one's earlier experiences;

3) *yu dang you meng,* dreams caused by great desires;

4) *yu fen bie meng,* dreams caused by separation; and

5) *yu zhu ming meng,* dreams caused by various diseases.

The Six Dreams *(liu meng)* Classification System

This categorization system for dreams was popular before and during the Qin dynasty, and was recorded in *The Rites of Zhou.* One may assume that the later Confucian editors of the book added material related to the Six Dreams system; however, it is known from extant sources that the system was indeed used by some dream-interpreting officials in the Zhou dynasty. Zhou interpreters not only utilized the Six Dreams classification for predictions of good and bad fortune, but they also utilized dreams in combination with astronomical calculations to predict natural phenomenon. These were used to determine the status of the kingdom, and had great influence on decisions made by the king. The Six Dreams were:

1) *zheng meng,* ordinary dreams. These were characterized as dreams forgotten after waking, and thus not disruptive to one's daily life.

They were felt to have taken place in a natural, peaceful, and quiet mood and held little consequence for decision-making;

2) *hao meng,* nightmares. Both surprising and shocking, these were seen as related to evil things or evil actions that the dreamer had been involved in before sleeping. Such dreams were often marked by the dreamer's groaning and screaming during sleep;

3) *si meng,* thinking dreams. These were of two types: a thinking dream while awake, and a thinking dream while asleep. Both were believed related to worries and anxieties, especially an excessive pre-occupation or obsession with some matter;

4) *wu meng,* transient-state dreams. These occurred while one was in a state between sleeping and being awake, more like what we call a day dream, but while the dreamer might feel that he was awake, he was in fact asleep;

5) *xi meng,* happy dreams. This dreams could be directly linked to pleasurable events, past or future, in the experience of the dreamer;

6) *ju meng,* fearful dreams. These were related directly to fears not unlike those that one experienced when awake.

The Nine Dreams *(jiu meng)* Classification System

The Ming dynasty author Chen Shi Yuan in *The Leisure and Pleasure of Interpreting Dreams (Meng Zhan Yi Zhi),* noted that there were nine reasons for an individual to have dreams and consequently there were nine ways to interpret those dreams. These are listed as follows:

1) *qi sheng.* Chen Shi Yuan's analysis was based on the established concept that too much air in the body, the condition of *qi sheng,* or "strong Qi," caused exciting dreams. He explained "If the Yin Qi is too strong, then one will dream that he is wading, crossing a big river and thus feels fear; if the Yang Qi is too much, then one will dream that there is a big bright fire; if both Yin Qi and Yang Qi are too much, then one will dream of killing and fighting. If the upper body Qi is strong, then one will dream of flying; if the lower body

Qi is strong, then one will dream of falling down. Being too hungry will lead to dreams of obtaining things; being too full will lead to dreams of giving things away. Strong liver Qi will lead to dreams of anger while strong lung Qi will lead to dreams of fear, flying, and crying. Strong heart Qi will lead to dreams of happiness, laughter, or fear while strong spleen Qi will lead to dreams of songs and music. Strong kidney Qi will lead to dreams of discomfort around waste. Too many short worms inside the stomach will lead to dreams of crows gathering together; too many long worms, on the other hand, will lead to dreams of fighting and injury. These dreams are caused by strong Qi, and they can be thus interpreted."

2) *qi xu.* Dreams instigated by this "weak Qi" were felt to be depressing, negative, pessimistic, and demeaning to the spirit. Chen explained that "If the lung Qi is weak, then one will dream of seeing white things (white being the color of death) or dreams of killing and blood." Other examples are given, such as, when the kidney Qi is weak, one will dream about boats sinking; when the kidney Qi is improving, one will dream of the boats or people floating upward. When the liver Qi is weak, one will dream of grass growing from germs; when the heart Qi is weak, one will have dreams of fire, and so on.

The causative factor here is Qi, the essence that links Yin and Yang, the five elements, and the five organs inside the human body. The concept of Qi as an operative agent is an important one in early Chinese philosophy, cosmology, and metaphysics. In each of these situations, external Qi is thought to invade the body and cause dreams. Since a balance of Yin Qi (strong or weak) and Yang Qi (strong or weak) is essential, any imbalance in any organ causes specific problems. These principles were first recorded in *The Book of Internal Medicine* and *The Book of Lie Zi.*

3) *xie yu.* This condition arises when external Qi invades various parts of the body and so leads to dreams relating to those parts. For example, if Qi invades the lungs, the person will dream of a strange metal (one of the five elements, associated with lungs). If Qi invades the liver, one would dream of forests (wood), while if Qi invades the kidneys, one will dream of falling from a cliff or sink-

ing into water. If the Qi invades the legs, one will dream of being unable to walk, perhaps mired in mud, while if the Qi invades the genitals, one will dream of urinating or defecating.

4) *ti zhi*. Both Chen Shi Yuan's book and *The Book of Lie Zi* explain that circumstances related to the sleeping environment influence one's dreams. For example, if one sleeps with something in his mouth, he dreams about speaking; if one sleeps with his feet bound, he dreams of climbing cliffs; if one's head is not on the pillow while sleeping, he dreams of falling down; if he sleeps on a rope, he dreams of snakes; if he wears colorful clothes, he dreams of a tiger or leopard; if he sleeps with tree branches or twigs in his hair, he dreams that he is upside down.

5) *qing yi*. This literally means dreams with emotions overflowing, said to be caused by an excess of anger, fear, happiness, etc., in the dreamer. Chen Shi Yuan explained "If one is extremely happy, in his dreams he will be open and free flowing; if he is worried, his dreams are closed and secretive; if he is sad, his dreams will be of seeking for help; if he is frightened, he will dream of madness."

6) *zhi ye*. These dreams exhibit a direct connection between the dream subject and everyday experience. This type of dream is the same as *zhi meng*, one of the Ten Dreams classified by Wang Fu in his *On Human Potentials (Qian Fu Lun)*. If one dreams of seeing a gentleman in his dream, for example, he will see a gentleman during the day; if one sees a deer in his dream, he will see a deer, etc.

7) *bi xiang*. In these dreams the symbolic relationship between the dream subject and real events are stressed, the former believed to portend the latter. For example, if one is going to be promoted, he will dream of a coffin, both words having the same sound, *kuan;* if one is going to make money, he will dream of something dirty, based on the belief that money is unclean; if one is going to become a nobleman, he will dream of climbing high; if one is going to become prosperous, he will dream of fish or rain, all having the same sound, *yu,* meaning abundance; if

disaster is coming, one will dream of white clothes, the color of death; if one is going to be blessed or become favored by a high ranking official, he will dream of fine clothes, and so on. Such dreams were felt to be subconscious expressions of future events.

8) *fan ji.* These dreams are characterized by the appearance of subjects or details that are just the opposite of their true meanings. If one is getting married, he will dream of crying; if one destined to weep, fight, or go to court, he will dream of singing and dancing; if one is cold, he will dream of warm things; if one is hungry, he will dream of being sated, etc. A story recorded in *The Book of Lie Zi* tells that Yin had servants working for him day and night. On and off he would have dreams of being king, and enjoying the pleasures of that position. In fact, however, he ran a large business, and pushed both himself and his servants tirelessly. As a result he was run down and weak all the time and felt himself a mere drone. As time passed he suffered some losses and was forced to endure the curses and abuse of others. Finally he took the advice of a friend and quite this tough position. He not only began to worry less, but also began treating his servants with dignity. Strangely, however, as his life improved, he began to have dreams of being a servant.

9) *li yao.* These dreams are caused by ghosts or monsters, who enter one's dreams and fill the dreamer with fear. This type of dream is directly related to the folk belief that the appearance of ghosts or monsters as a result of the dreams can predict disasters or portend unfortunate happenings. The desire to rid oneself of such dreams led, during the Qin and Han periods, to a formal ritual called *qu gui,* meaning "expelling ghosts."

The Ten Dreams *(shi meng)* Classification System

This system of dream categorization is recorded in Wang Fu's book, *On Human Potentials,* said to have been written in the Eastern Han dynasty. Wang Fu explained each of the categories in his Ten Dreams system as follows:

1) *zhi meng*. Literally, these are straight (direct) dreams. In this category, the dream subject and the future of the dreamer are directly related. For example, in the Zhou dynasty, before emperor Yu was born, his mother dreamed that the Heavenly Emperor told her, "Name your son Yu, and give him the Tang state to rule." After her son was born, his palm-print revealed the character *yu*.

2) *xiang meng*. These are symbolic dreams, portending connections to real object or events as regarded by folk beliefs or drawn from early texts. For example, verses in the *Book of Songs* state, "The bear is the symbol of male; the worm and snake are the symbols of female," and that "Lots of fish means abundance and plenty; lots of flags mean prosperity for the house."

3) *jing meng*. If the dreamer is focused on a particular subject, it will no doubt become the subject of a dream. It is said that Confucius thought of the virtues of emperor Wu Wang and thus had dreams of the virtues he practiced. Wang Fu's *jing meng* classification is similar to the *si meng* (thinking dream) type in the Six Dreams classification scheme from *The Rites of Zhou*.

4) *xiang meng*. If one does something intently during the daytime, he will continue the activity in his dreams. For example, if one worries about a business arrangement during his daily activities, he will surely dream of it during the night.

5) *ren meng*. Wang Fu indicates that the meaning of dreams differ depending upon the fortune, position, status, gender, and age of the human dreamer. For example, if a good person dreams of something, it may mean bad fortune while if an evil person dreams of the identical thing, it may mean good fortune. And what might be a glorious dream for a rich person might portend disaster for a poor person.

6) *gan meng*. In this category the weather or climate is reflected in dreams. For example, dreams about gloomy and rainy weather can inspire in the dreamer feelings of gloom and depression, while dreams about dryness and drought will make one unable to con-

centrate. On extremely cold days, dreams may make people feel sad or sorrowful while dreams on days with strong winds will make people feel elated or invigorated.

7) *shi meng*. Literally, "time dreams," *shi meng* reflect the change of seasons. For example, dreams in the spring will be about planting or growing; dreams in the summer will be about brightness and heat; dreams in the autumn and winter will be about harvest and storage. These dream subjects were felt to be directly related to the seasonal matters in life, and thus a reflection of the operations of the five elements.

8) *fan meng*. As in the nine-dream system, these dreams include subject matter or details that are just the opposite of the situation in real, waking life. For example, Jin Wen Gong, the king of Jin, dreamed that he was captured by the king of Chu, who proceeded to eat his brain with salt. When he awoke he was greatly disturbed, thinking that this dream was an omen of what was to come. But instead, he fought bravely and won the battle against Chu.

9) *bing meng*. In these "sickness dreams" one dreams of the illness he has or will get. Disease caused by the Yin elements will lead to dreams about cold; disease caused by the Yang elements will lead to dreams about heat. Internal disease will lead to dreams of disordered organs; external disease will lead to dreams of swelling and edema. Dreams caused by diseases are considered either "scattering" (indicating loss of focus, abilities, mental clarity, etc.) or "concentrating" (indicating tenseness, anxiety, etc.). Wang Fu adopted these medical principles from *The Book of Internal Medicine*.

10) *xing meng*. The dreams of this group portend outcomes that are dependent upon the character or personality of the dreamer. For example, one who has good temper or character generally has dreams portending good fortune; one who has a bad temper or evil nature will usually have evil dreams. Each dream, however, must be interpreted with regard to individual circumstances, and it is further pointed out that frequent interpretations of dreams of this type can make them inaccurate.

The Five No-Interpreting *(wu bu zhan)* Dream Theory

This theory identifies five conditions under which dreams cannot or should not be interpreted. It is based on criteria which were set forth in the early dynasties and recorded subsequently in Chen Shi Yuan's *Meng Zhan Yi Zhi,* written in the Ming dynasty. According to this text, dreams are interpreted primarily to reveal the will of the gods and therefore are not something to be taken lightly. This reinforces our understanding that dream interpretation among the ancient Chinese was regarded as serious business indeed. Chen further states that when interpreting dreams the interpreter should be totally loyal to the identified principles. If one adheres to these principles, the resulting interpretations will stand the test of truthfulness and be found to correctly predict the future. Although these principles were for interpreters, dreamers were also supposed to follow them before going to the interpreters. It was advised that dreams which took place under the following conditions were not to be interpreted:

1) Dreams during times of mental instability, such as dreams that take place when one is extremely frightened or distracted with bereavement;

2) Dreams that occur when one is terribly worried;

3) Dreams that occur when one is in a state of "twilight sleep," that is, not completely asleep and with feelings of foreboding;

4) Dreams from which a person is awakened and thus unable to complete the dream;

5) Completed dreams about which the dreamer cannot remember the entire dream or its outcome.

The Five No-Examining *(wu bu yan)* Dream Theory

Supportive to the above theory, five "no-examining" conditions were identified under which dream interpretations were considered to be unreliable or unable to be proved. These five conditions, which related to the skills or methods of the interpreter, are as follows:

1) If the interpreter does not know the channel or movement of the spirits;

2) If the interpreter is not an expert or does not know the art of interpreting dreams;

3) If the interpreter does not wholeheartedly believe in the principles of interpreting dreams he will be unaware of the heavenly meaning of dreams. If he is not qualified, the interpretations will not be true;

4) If the interpreter approaches the business of interpreting too casually or playfully;

5) If the interpreter expresses a contradictory or ambiguous interpretation, then it is not true.

The Body-Closing *(bi xing)* State

A creation of the Daoists and first recorded in the *Book of Zhuang Zi,* the body-closing state is a concept that helps distinguish a sleeping dream from a daydream. The term *bi xing* literally describes a state in which all the doors and windows of the body are closed to the outside, thus enabling one to have true dreams. Body opening *(xing kai)* has the opposite meaning, referring to the doors and windows to the body being open, i.e., when one is awake and his functions directed toward the outside world. A well-known philosopher, Zhang Zai of the Northern Song dynasty, further explained this concept in the book *On Enlightenment.* He noted that when one is asleep and is in the body-closing state, his "Qi is functioning internally." Qi, the essence of the body, accommodates the movement of the spirits.

The Arts of Dream Interpretation *(zhan meng shu)*

Besides the ways of classifying and interpreting dreams promulgated by the specific individuals listed here, other principles are used in interpreting dreams, including methods based on various philosophical or cosmological views in vogue at various times in Chinese history. These cover a wide range of systems and methods and here are collectively referred to as "arts of dream interpretation."

As early as the Shang dynasty, tortoise shells were used in divination and dream interpretation. The shells were placed in or near a fire causing them to crack, and the lines of cracking were utilized in dream interpretation as well as general prognostication. According to *The Rites of Zhou*, the Tai Pu was in charge of interpreting tortoise shells, interpreting "changes" (*yi*), and interpreting dreams as well; astrological systems were incorporated into dream interpretations during this period. Interpreters of later dynasties summarized these early methods and developed them into a comprehensive art of interpreting dreams. Dream interpretation became an independent art with a distinctive focus and perspective, and widely practiced, most often in accord with one of the following ten methods:

1) *meng xie yu pu,* dreams supported by predictions. This method integrated fortune-telling into the process of dream interpretation. In the Zhou dynasty, tortoise shells were used, as were the eight trigrams, or *ba gua*. These were used to ascertain the will of the spirits and to predict good or ill fortune. This method of interpreting dreams is recorded in one of the earliest documents of classical literature, *The Book of Shang (Shang Shu)*. It is written, for example, that emperor Wu Wang of the Zhou dynasty was trying to defeat emperor Zou of the Shang dynasty. He called a meeting of his court officials and requested that a dream he had had be interpreted. The dream he described was seen as reflecting the virtues of his people in their struggle against the Shang, and an exhortation to them to be strong and to fight with diligence. The dream interpreter stressed that it was their moral duty to fight against their enemies, a heavenly inspired message and a portent of victory.

2) *ri yue xing chen zhan meng,* the use of the sun, moon, and stars to interpret dreams. In this important early method, recorded in both *The Rites of Zhou* and *The Grand History*, dreams were interpreted according to celestial phenomenon. In the former it is written that "To interpret dreams, it is necessary to know well the annual calendar. The joining points (moments) of the sky and the earth should be observed and the Yin and Yang air should be distinguished so that the good or ill omens of the six dream types can

be interpreted according to the movement of the sun, moon, and stars." *The Grand History* records that in the second year of his reign, during the latter part of the Zhou dynasty, king Yuan of Song called the scholar Wei Ping and said "I had a dream in which I saw a man whose neck and head were long. He was dressed in colorful silk clothes and rode in a beautiful black horse cart. He said, 'I am the messenger of the rivers and seas and came to let you know that something has blocked my way. Although I wish to pass through, I cannot. Since you are the king, I came to tell you of this problem.' What does this dream mean?"

Before answering, the scholar set up his equipment and observed the light of the moon and the position of the Great Bear, locating the direction of the sun, and dividing the four dimensions and the eight directions. He divined a turtle-shaped animal and told the king: "According to the heavens, the main star of our country is in Altar, and is gathering with other stars. It is the time for souls and ghosts to meet. The river goes straight from the north to the south and now is the time for the river to swell. The south wind is coming and thus indicates flooding of the river. The white clouds surrounding the river and the handle of the dipper (the Great Bear) pointing to the sun both indicate that captured people need to be rescued. The man in the cart is in fact the image of the turtle." The king immediately ordered an investigation into the truth of this interpretation and found that there were captured countrymen of Song who indeed needed to be rescued. Thus, the prediction was found to be true.

3) *wu xing ba gua zhan meng,* using the five elements and the eight trigrams to interpret dreams. This method of interpreting dreams utilizes the movement and relationship between and among the five elements (water, wood, fire, earth, and metal) and eight trigrams (*qian*—heaven, *kun*—earth, *kan*—water, *li*—fire, *zhen*—thunder, *gen*—mountain, *xun*—wind, *dui*—swamp). The five elements are believed both to generate (or support) and to destroy (or restrain) each other. Water generates wood, wood generates fire, fire generates earth, earth generates metal, and metal generates water. Meanwhile, water destroys fire, fire destroys metal, metal destroys wood, wood destroys earth, and earth destroys water. This con-

stant, balanced movement of these elements is operative in both the universe and the human body. Philosophers use them to explain the origin and movement of the world; medical doctors use them to describe the organic system within human body; fortune-tellers use them to predict an individual's fate or luck.

The eight diagrams is a divination system developed as early as the Zhou dynasty, in which a single line (Yang) or broken line (Yin) represents male or female elements, respectively. Each are said to be meaningfully related and mutually generative, and a combination of three lines (*yao*) is called a trigram. Heaven, earth, water, fire, thunder, mountain, wind, and swamp are each represented by a one of these combinations. The universe is represented by the 64 possible pairings of these trigrams. As the eight diagrams alone are too simple to explain everything in any detail, sages combined two of each together to form diagrams with six *yao;* thus sixty-four diagrams (8 times 8) and three hundred eighty-four *yao* (64 times 6) were generated. In this way, the combination and movement of Yin and Yang within each diagram were believed able to provide clear explanations about everything in nature and in human society. It is said that Confucius edited the *The Book of Change,* adding his own explanations about each *yao* and diagram.

A story in *The Book of Jin* tells that when Fu Rong was governor, there was a person named Dong Feng who had returned home after three years of traveling and studying. The night of his return, Dong stayed with his wife at the home of her parents; that very night, his wife was killed. The wife's parents suspected that Dong had committed this crime and had him arrested. Dong suffered so greatly from the beatings of his interrogators that he could no longer tolerate the pain, and confessed that he killed his wife. When Fu Rong heard of this story, he thought it strange and interviewed Dong. Dong told him that before he got home, he had a dream in which he was riding a horse and came to a river. He started to cross the river from the north bank, heading to the south, but in the middle of the river, the horse stopped. He kept whipping the horse, but the horse refused to move. He looked down and saw two suns in the water, on the left side a sun white and wet, and on the right side, a sun black and dry. He awoke quite distraught, thinking the dream an ill omen. He went to a dream interpreter who told him that he would have an encounter with the law and told him not to sleep on his pillow and not to wash his hair. When he got home, his wife warmed water for him to wash his hair and gave him a pillow. Dong remembered the interpreter's words and did not use the water or the pillow. His wife then washed her hair and went to sleep on the pillow. That was the night she was killed.

Fu Rong interpreted the dream using the eight trigrams. According to *The Book of Change*, water means "male" and horse means "female"; the two suns in the water indicate one wife and two husbands. Since water (*kan*) also means "law" and is on the top, and the horse (*li*) is at the bottom according to its nature, he reasoned that Dong should live. Emperor Wen Wang of the Zhou dynasty once dreamed of the same trigram and survived imprisonment. Fu Rong further reasoned that since the character *feng* is composed of "water" on the left and "horse" on the right, and the character *chang* is composed of two "suns," the murderer must be someone named Feng Chang. A person named Feng Chang was later arrested and confessed that he and Dong's wife planned to do away with her husband. He was to sneak into their bedroom and kill Dong, recognizing him in the moonlight by the fact that he was resting on a pillow with newly washed hair. As it turned out, however, Dong heeded the warning of his dream and his wife was murdered instead.

4) *zhi jie zhang meng*, direct association used to interpret dreams. Dreams in this category are considered directly related to what one experiences in real life. *On Eternity* says, "People may have direct dreams. One dreams of seeing a person A and a person B, then he sees both A and B the next day. This is a direct dream." To some extent, this kind of dream needs only to be related and does not need interpretation. A story in the book *Speech Garden* tells that Di Qing, the well-known black-faced Judge Bao of the Song dynasty, had a dream when he was the governor of Chen Zhou in which he saw prime minister Cai Que on the list of ancestors names in the Zhan Xu Temple. At that time, Cai Que had just passed the provincial civil examination. Di Qing told Cai Que of his dream, and encouraged Cai Que to study harder. Later Cai Que did indeed become the prime minister under emperor Shenzong.

Chen Shi Yuan quotes a story from *The Book of the Five Dynasties* in which the king of latter Liang, Chu You Mu, in an effort to usurp the throne of emperor Mo sent a killer to emperor Mo's bedroom. Emperor Mo was sound asleep, but dreamed of a killer coming to him and woke up, startled. Hearing the killer draw a sword from its sheath, he shouted and leaped up to protect himself. The killer was apprehended.

5) *fan shi zhan meng,* using opposite meanings to interpret dreams. Basically, if one dreams about something bad, good will happen, and vice versa. This was a popular method in ancient times, but applied only in specific situations and contexts, probably to meet the obvious psychological needs of the dreamers and the practical needs of interpreters. *The Book of Zuo* records that when the countries of Jin and Chu were in battle, the king of Jin dreamed that the king of Chu was lying on Jin's body and sucking out his brains. Although he feared that this dream was a grave omen, his interpreter pointed out that the king of Jin was lying facing the sky, a gesture of winning heaven, while the king of Chu was lying face down, a gesture of supplication and punishment. This indicated that the Chu had become subjects of the Jin. The next day, the Jin army fought a fierce battle and defeated the Chu.

The Book of Zhuang Zi says that, "A person who dreams of drinking wine will cry later; a person who dreams of crying will be successful in the hunt." In *The Remaining Books from Dunhuang*, it records that "One who dreams of one's death will have longevity; a dream of crying will brings happy things." And *The New Collection of Zhou Gong's Dream Interpretations* says: "A dream of sick people is a good omen; a dream of family graves is extremely auspicious; a dream of finding treasure portends one's fortune will be lost."

6) *xiang zheng zhan meng,* using symbolic meanings to interpret dreams. Perhaps this was the most frequently used method of interpreting dreams in ancient times. For example, if the sun appeared in a dream, it had the meaning that one would meet or see the emperor, as the sun symbolized the emperor while the moon symbolized the empress. In Wang Fu's *On Human Potentials,* he refers to *The Book of Songs,* saying, "Bears and such are the signs of the

male; worms and snakes are the signs of the female. Fish and fruit indicate an abundant harvest; various flags are signs of household prosperity. These are dream symbols." Of course, symbolic associations from ancient times must be adjusted to incorporate the dream objects of today. For example, cars, bicycles, and electric lights did not exist in the early days, but may have the same symbolic associations as horse carts, horse riding, or candles.

7) *guan lian zhan meng,* using object association to interpret dreams. This refers to the interpretation of dreams by associating them to related objects. The *Tai Ping Yu Lan* tells that, "Dreaming of a dining table means that guests are coming. A big table would mean more guests and a small table would mean fewer guests." *The Collection of Literary Essays* gives this example: "A person has a dream in which he sees a stove. This means that he is worried about marrying a woman or marrying out his daughter. Why is it so? Because a stove indicates a female." *The New Collection of Zhou Gong's Dream Interpretations* records that "If one dreams of looking into a mirror, it means someone is coming; seeing ill people taking a bath is a bad omen; seeing a reed mat in a dream means the dreamer is worried about being ill." This method relates the dream details to practical beliefs to determine dream meanings. For example, a reed mat was often used when a dying person was moved from a regular bed, and thus is associated with death. This practice is recorded in *The Book of Rites.*

8) *xie yin zhan meng,* use of homonyms to interpret dreams. This method of interpreting dreams has its basis in relating words with the same pronunciation and is possibly unique to China. An example in *The New Collection of Zhou Gong's Dream Interpretations* says, "Seeing shoes in dreams means that everything will be in harmony," because shoes and harmony are both pronounced *xie.* This method was widely practiced among the common people. As an example, the word for "eyes" has the same pronunciation as "feelings" so eyes and feelings are associated. Chinese businessmen do not like the word *she* (tongue) for it has a pronunciation similar to the word for "to wear out." For boat people, saying the word *chen* is taboo, for its pronunciation could be either a family name or "to

sink." Similarly, *guan cai* meaning "coffin" sounds the same as the words for "official" and "treasure."

References to such connections can be found in numerous books throughout the centuries. *Random Notes of the Qing Xiang Studio* tells that one Li Di had a long and beautiful beard. Before he was to take the highest-level test in the civil service examination system, he had a dream in which his chin was shaved clean. Although he felt extremely agitated after waking up, a dream interpreter told him that this dream was an omen that he would take first place in the upcoming examination. He explained that the top candidate in Li's province was named Liu Zi, a homonym for "keeping beard," so Li's dream of being shaved (*ti zi*, a homonym for "replacing Zi") indicated that Li Di would take Liu Zi's top position in the examination. Li Di indeed won first place.

9) *jie zi zhan meng*, using character analysis to interpret dreams. This method interprets a dream by analyzing the characters for each word of the dream subject. For example, if one dreams about money, an analysis of the character for money will reveal the meaning of the dream.

The Book of Jin records the following two stories about the dream interpreter, Suo Chen. Once Suo Chen dreamed he saw a captured soldier come to him with his upper body naked. He noted that the character for capture, *lu*, without its upper part would mean male, *nan*. He reasoned the dream meant that his wife would give birth to a son. This came to be true. The second story tells of one named Zhang Miao, who was sent out as a messenger, and dreamed his feet were bitten by a wolf. Suo Chen said that if the "meat" part of the character for "feet" is taken away, then the remaining part would be the character for "give up." Thus he interpreted this strange dream to mean that his mission would not be accomplished. Later, it turned out that the man betrayed his master and message was never delivered.

10) *fan qie zhan meng*, using combinations of syllables to interpret dreams. This method of interpreting dreams uses relationships between pronunciation of words, which, in ancient times, were pronounced differently than today. This method involved taking

the consonant of the first word and the vowel of the second word, thus forming another word from the recombined parts. It should be noted that this method of building words is no longer used in modern Chinese interpreting. The same principle was also used in reassembling the radicals and phonetics, the two graphic elements of most Chinese characters.

Notes from Youyang tells that a man named Li Bo purchased a hundred *dou* (a unit of dry grain, one deciliter) of rice and sent his brother with a boat to fetch it. However the brother did not return at the appointed time. That night Li Bo dreamed he saw a white horse being washed (*xi bai ma*). He went to see Mei Bo Cheng, a well-known dream interpreter, who thought for a long time and then explained that the written characters *xi ma* (washing horse) can be reassembled to mean "water falling, running stomach" *(xie)*, while *ma xi* (horse-washing) can be made into "rice" *(mi)*. Thus "washing a white horse" can be interpreted to mean "falling white rice." He reasoned that this dream indicated that a strong windstorm had turned the boat over, and that the rice had fallen into the water. Days later, his brother returned home empty-handed, and stated that the boat had been turned over in a storm and all the rice lost.

Lucky Dreams *(ji meng)*

Highly influenced by Buddhist beliefs, lucky dreams were said to be those involving cleanliness, brightness, good health, prosperity, freshness, and happiness. Lucky dreams are recorded in Wang Fu's *On Human Potentials,* and are discussed at great length in *The New Collection of Zhou Gong's Dream Interpretations* and Chen Shi Yuan's *Meng Zhan Yi Zhi.* The meanings of these dreams, however, are not simply revealed by direct interpretation. Wang Fu said in his book that "The same dream for the noble and rich may mean something different from that of the poor and humble . . . Each dream has to be judged according to the individual's condition." Chen Shi Yuan further wrote that "Evil people may have a dream with lucky content, but it may still be an ill omen, for the luck cannot be realized. After all, it does not matter if a dream is seen as an ill omen or a good omen, it is the dreamer himself who finalizes the nature of the dream."

The Disastrous Dream *(xiong meng)*

This direct opposite of the lucky dream can also be translated as the inauspicious dream. It was also highly influenced by Buddhist belief and is mentioned in Wang Fu's *On Human Potentials*. The dream content of a disastrous dream related to killing, robbing, prostitution, uncleanliness, falling, declining, and so on. Influenced by the Buddhist concept of karma, such inauspicious dreams were even thought to have their origins in earlier generations of the dreamer's family; dreamers were thus suffering for the sins of their ancestors.

The *New Collection of Zhou Gong's Dream Interpretations* says that, "In dreams, seeing the sun and the moon disappearing is evil; seeing clothes stained with dirt or excrement is evil; seeing trees dying is an omen of the disease or death of one's mother; seeing someone lying in a well is evil; seeing new socks is lucky but seeing torn or worn socks is bad; seeing teeth falling out is inauspicious." However, the inauspicious dream can also be auspicious under circumstances calling for opposite interpretation. Similarly, the real meaning of the inauspicious dream would depend upon the virtue or lack thereof in the dreamer. Cautious and correct behavior can help one avoid bad luck and turn it into good luck. Thus, as recorded in the same book, "In dreams, seeing excrement or dirty clothes may be a great lucky omen; seeing a coffin being carried into the house may bring great fortune." Chen Shi Yuan said that "Lucky or virtuous people have disastrous or evil dreams, but these dreams, though inauspicious in content, may not necessarily be so, and the evils can be avoided."

Praying for Lucky Dreams *(qi meng)*

From earliest times, the practice of praying for lucky dreams was popular both in the court and in common life. The nature of dreams, whether lucky or evil, was considered to be a decision of the gods and spirits. Fearful of disastrous dreams, people prayed to the gods for lucky dreams. *The Rites of Zhou* contains details of rituals practiced by the Zhou emperors to solicit lucky dreams. A Ming history records that there was a temple for He Gu (one of the eight immortals) in the north of Fujian province where before the civil service examinations, local students and scholars would pray for their success in the examinations and for dreams which bore good omens.

The Evil-Avoiding Dream *(rang meng)*

The rituals practiced to avoid evil or disastrous dreams were more complicated than those for soliciting lucky dreams. The practice of these rituals originated as early as the Shang dynasty, and the tortoiseshell and bone inscriptions of that dynasty testify to such practices.

The New Collection of Zhou Gong's Dream Interpretations contains a chapter on avoiding disastrous dreams, and lists various charms and spells to help avoid them. The use of the charms was explained: "Those who have evil dreams at night should not tell anyone else when they get up in the morning. Calm your heart and write down what is on this page with black ink, then put it safely under your bed and do not let others know about it. The text of the curse goes: 'Red sunshine, the sun rises in the east. This charm breaks the hold of the dream and expels evil. Read it three times and all ghosts will flee. Its effect is as a command. All evil dreams have the surname of Yun (cloud) and personal name Xinggui (traveling ghost); all evil ideas have the surname of Jia (false) and personal name Zizhi (self straightening), or the surname of Zi (son) and formal personal name Shihu (a kind of plant), I know your surname and personal name. Get a thousand miles away from me, immediately! Go!'"

A Complete Collection of Books of All Eras records that having frequent evil dreams is due to ghosts or evil spirits. To avoid such dreams and to turn them into lucky dreams, one should pinch one's philtrum (the area under the nose and above upper lip) with one's left hand from two to seven times and click one's upper teeth with one's lower teeth from two to seven times. Waking up with lucky dreams, one should rub one's eyes and click one's teeth from two to seven time.

The Dream God *(meng shen)*

The dream god drives away evil dreams and brings lucky dreams, and thus manages *hun* and *po,* the two souls residing in each living person. When a person dies, the two souls are separated, and the *hun* rises to the sky while the *po* stays with the dead body. In order to keep the dead and the living at peace, the deceased's *hun* and *po* must be united. The *hun* is often considered a good soul that can transform into an ancestral spirit or sage spirit to be worshiped at the family alter. The *po* is generally a bad soul that can transform into a ghost or spirit with the dead body. All the fearful stories about ghosts and graveyards are about this bad soul.

The *Poetry of Chu* states that under the Heavenly Emperor is a god in charge of dreams who puts the separate souls *hun* and *po* together into the body. *Notes from the Zhixu Studio,* written in the Tang dynasty, states that the name of this dream god is Zhi Li. If one calls his name before going to sleep, one will then have fresh, beautiful, happy, lucky dreams.

The *Tong Dian* records that in the latter Han dynasty, a ritual of driving away evil ghosts was performed every winter on the tenth day before the last month of the lunar calendar. The ritual consisted of one hundred and twenty males chosen from noble families, wearing red hats and black clothes, holding ritual objects in their hands while surrounding twelve beasts (masked men), and singing together: "Bo Qi eating dreams." This is an example of taking Bo Qi as a dream god eating evil dreams.

A Complete Collection of Books of All Eras records that there is a temple in the Chengdu area of today's Sichuan Province where students and scholars go to pray for lucky dreams. The prayers take place inside the temple where there is a mural depicts a woman holding daisy flowers while facing a monkey. It is said that all prayers to her magically come true.

The Dream Ghost *(meng gui)*

The dream ghost is said to be able to make people have evil and inauspicious dreams. *The Rites of Zhou* records a ritual called *nan ou yi,* the purpose of which was to get rid of the dream ghost. Various dream curses for this purpose are recorded throughout history. *A Complete Collection of Books of All Eras* tells the story of a dream-eating monster who enjoys devouring human dreams. It never closes its mouth and usually waits for those who tell their dreams in the morning. Since the good and ill omens of a dream depend on the dreamer's telling, people are cautioned to describe their dreams carefully. Today's taboo on relating dreams early the next morning may well originate from this belief. Song dynasty texts give the creature the name Shi Meng Shou, the dream-eating monster, and claim that the dream ghost may also eat the dreamer.

The Dream Curse *(meng zhou)*

This is a way of utilizing curses to rid oneself of evil dreams or to change ill omens into good omens, a concept related to those of "praying for lucky dreams" and "evil-avoiding dreams" above. Although practiced by some Buddhists, most of the known dream curses are from the Daoist sources. There are curses to cause dreams, curses to get rid of dreams, curses for lucky dreams, and curses for bad dreams. It is said that only the monks or dream interpreters know the special chants used to rid one of evil dreams as dream curses are rarely documented in writing. *Random Notes of the Cloud Immortal* tells of a "golden ring curse" *(jin lun zhou):* "By tapping the two earlobes and eating a heart-comforting pill while reading or reciting the golden ring curse, one will have dreams that night about the person being thought of, whether the person is alive or dead."

The Notes from the Zhixu Studio gives examples of dream curses but they are the transliterations from sounds of the curses to sounds from Buddhist scriptures, so that gradually the original meanings have been lost. However, reciting the various spells, charms, and curses are essential practices for Daoists and this is one reason why more Daoist curses exist. Before and after reading or reciting the curses, one is directed to rub the philtrum for 14 times (2 x 7), bite or click the teeth 14 times (2 x 7), or rub the eyes and swallow saliva 27 times (3 x 9). These practices are based on significant Daoist numbers and are related to arts of promoting health and extending longevity. One of the key texts of Daoism, *Yun Ji Qi Jian*, contains curses for avoiding evil dreams and praying for lucky dreams, and special curses for Daoist monks.

Dream Grass *(meng cao)*

This refers to using a special grass or drug to pray for dreams and to predict good fortune or bad for the dreamer. Because this special grass or drug is directed to be held on the chest, it is sometimes called "chest grass." During the reign of emperor Wu of the Han dynasty, a celebrated minister named Dongfang Shuo obtained this grass and dedicated it to the emperor, who held it on his chest when sleeping. According to *The Book on the Relations of Matters,* the dream grass grows in the cold north and looks like the cattail but is red in color. One of its unique qualities is that during the daytime, its leaves shrink and are quite small. It is recorded that if one holds the dream grass on one's chest while sleeping, one's dreams can be interpreted immediately. A similar record is also found in *Notes from Youyang*.

The Dream Bird *(meng niao)*

According to *The Book of Mountains and Seas* this bird, used to rid one of evil dreams, looks like a crow, but has three heads and three tails, and a five-colored crown. Called a *qiyu*, it is good at imitating the sound of laughing. Eating this bird will help people get rid of bad dreams and protect them from evil. *The Book of Songs* says, "The dream bird is the phoenix."

The Dream Worm *(meng chong)*

The dream worm is an animal of the type called *peng yue*, and is said to have the ability to travel between dreams and human beings. According to the *Sou Shen Ji*, this creature lives on the seashore and looks like a crab but is much smaller. It often reports dreams to people and calls itself *chang qing*, so people living along the coast call it by that name.

Similar is the Daoist concept of the Three Worm Gods *(san shi)*, documented in the books *You Yang Za Zu* and *Yun Ji Qi Jian*. This theory holds that there are three worms, Peng Ju, Peng Zhi, Peng Jiao, also called respectively Qing Gu (Black Lady), Bai Gu (White Lady), and Xue Gu (Blood Lady). These three control the inside of the human body and therefore can remember people's wrong doings and report them to the Heavenly Emperor when the people are asleep. This idea emanates from the concepts of *hun* (the good soul) and *po* (the bad soul, or ghost) that brings bad dreams. Only those who practice Daoist principles are said to be able to rid themselves of the control of the three worms. The *Yun Ji Qi Jian* states that the upper worm god lives three inches behind the forehead, the middle worm god is behind the heart, and the lower worm god is three and three quarter inches behind the navel. Further, "The upper worm is keen on gems; the middle worm is interested in delicious food; the lower worm enjoys sexual activity."

The birth of Zhang Zhi He was foretold by his mother's dream of a maple tree growing in her abdomen (Wang).

PART TWO

Dream Symbols
and their
Interpretations

Ancestors

A dream of one's ancestors carries messages from them.

In these dreams, parents, grandparents, or ancestors of an earlier generation appear. Ancestor worship taught that when people died, their spirits did not die but could associate or make contact with the souls of the living. Through this contact of souls, the dead could support or help later, living generations.

The *Book of Zuo* tells the story of two countries, Qi and Jin, at war. The night before a major battle Han Jue, the general of Qi, had a dream in which his father appeared and told him that in the fighting on the coming day he should avoid the positions of left and right. General Han Jue followed the advice and was victorious in his battle with the Jin. However, arrows killed all those on the left and right sides of his chariot.

Another story from *The Book of Jin* tells that king Mu of the Southern Yan did not have a son. While seriously ill, he had a dream in which his father told him that he should give his crown to his niece, and by doing so others would not be enraged by jealousy, which would offer him protection. After he awoke, he followed his father's instructions given to him in the dream and entitled his niece as the future ruler.

Animals

See Bear, Cat, Cow, Deer, Dog, Dragon, Elephant, Frog, Hedgehog, Horse, Lion, Pig, Qilin, Snake, Tiger, Turtle, and Wolf

Bamboo

Bamboo dreams have a variety of symbolic meanings, from conflict to strength.

Interpreters derived different meanings from the actual natural characteristics of bamboo. For example, bamboo grows in sections called *jie*, a word with several meanings in Chinese, one being complicated or messy, as in *zuo jie* (to make knots, i.e., to complicate matters). Bamboo dreams are sometimes omens of impending quarrels. One text says, "Dreams of cutting bamboo trees mean verbal confrontation," while another records that "*Jie*, the sections of bamboo, are constraints, limits. Therefore, dreams of bamboo sections or joints mean that one possesses dignity or is a hermit."

In the *Tai Ping Yu Lan*, it states "Dreaming of bamboo means someone is worrying about matters." New bamboo is called *sun*, the same pronunciation as the word for premature death or damage. So a dream of new bamboo carries the meaning that a mother is worried. It is not a good omen. Thus it is said, "Dreams of new bamboo indicate worries that something bad will happen."

Bear

An omen that a son will be born who will be successful.

Although the bear can be a violent beast, interpreters believed that dreaming of a bear was a omen of good luck, meaning that a noble boy would be born. In the *Book of Songs*, a poem tells that a nobleman or sage dreaming of a bear foretold a noble boy entering the family; a dream of a snake, on the other hand, foretold the birth of a female child.

The *Book of Jin* relates the story of Fu Jian, the third son of emperor Hong Di. His mother, the empress, dreamed that one night while sitting in her chambers, pregnant, she saw a bear sitting at her door. At the conclusion of the dream she actually became pregnant. A boy was born to the empress named Fu Jian, who as interpreters foretold, became powerful and established his own kingdom, becoming the first emperor of Qi.

Red Bear
Visions of a red bear have various meanings.
A vision of the bear appearing through a screen means
that a disease is present but no great harm will come.

A red bear appearing in a dream is recorded in the *Tai Ping Yu Lan*. While suffering from what he thought was a minor illness, emperor Ping Gong of Jin dreamed of a read bear looking at him through a screen. He asked the well-known interpreter Zi Chan if this was an evil omen, but Zi Chuan replied that it represented the god Gong Gong, who was transformed into a bear after being defeated by Zhuan Xu. The significance of the red bear depended upon where it was seen. If the bear appeared in the hall the world would be in peace; if outside the hall, the world should be frightened. If the bear were seen at the door, ministers should worry, while if seen in the yard there would be no danger. If the bear were seen looking at the emperor through a screen, it meant that there is illness present but not of a serious nature. By offering sacrifices to Gong Gong and Zhuan Xu, all harm could be easily averted. The emperor did as instructed and subsequently recovered from his illness.

Yellow Bear
A dream that predicts one will be future ruler.

We have seen that a dream of a bear portends the birth of a son. As yellow is the color associated with the emperor, a dream or vision of a yellow bear brings additional rejoicing, as it foretells the birth of a future ruler.

The *Zuo Quan* tells the story of emperor Qin Gong, who had a dream of a yellow bear entering his bedroom. The bear was an incarnation of the future emperor Gun, who became great and powereful ruler.

Beard

An omen that one's destiny is positive.

Scholars and learned men have always been pictured as older men with long beards, and dreaming of a beard portends success in scholarship. Since in traditional China success in the state examinations was the way to an official position, such a dream also foretold financial success.

A beard increasing in length also indicates that great fortune is one's destiny. This symbolism is related to a well-known story of Yuan Zhong Dao of the Ming dynasty, who dreamed his beard grew two additional inches. A short time later, he was awarded a higher position.

See also Shaving

Beheading

**A dream of death or failure to attain
the highest success one can achieve.**

Wu Chu Hou of the Song dynasty recorded the story of being beheaded in a dream in *Qing Xiang Za Ji*. The story tells that a prime minister of the Song dynasty named Liu Kang had a dream in which someone beheaded him. While puzzled and frightened by this dream, he subsequently placed second in the civil service examinations. The dream was interpreted as an omen of failure to achieve the highest honor.

Having one's head severed in a dream can also foretell of coming death. The *Ji Yi Zhi* records the story of Zhu Shi Long, who was the minister of education. While he and his wife were both taking a nap one day, she dreamed that she saw a man carrying her husband's head out of the house. This dream was so vivid that she when she awoke she went to his bedroom and to her surprise found Zhu Shi asleep. When he awoke, his wife told him the dream and he remarked that it was indeed strange. Deeply frightened, he sought the interpretation of others, but not long after he was killed.

Bee (Mr. Thin Loin)

A dream of bees (or Mr. Thin Loin) portends prosperity.

The *Jiang Guan Ji* records that in the Qing dynasty a prostitute named Wu Cun Chi dreamed that she slept with a scholar. She asked the scholar his name, to which he responded, "Mr. Thin Loin." She had the same dream over and over for many nights, until one evening she dreamed that after having sex with Mr. Thin Loin, he became smaller and smaller and finally turned into a bee. The bee flew into the flowers of her garden, but she caught it and brought it into the house for safekeeping. She fed it and took care of it and it began to attract other bees, thousands of them. Soon they began to produce honey, which she sold in town and thus became quite prosperous. Thus a dream of bees or of "Mr. Thin Loin" became an omen of prosperity.

Bell

A dream of a bell predicts good luck.

A story in the Tang dynasty text *Xuan Shi Zhi* tells that one Qing Jiang Jun Sou was an old man who herded sheep in the fields with his sons. One day, he heard a strange voice coming out of the earth and both he and the boys ran away. Soon the old man had a dream of seeing another old man wearing black clothes, who said, "You must move me to Kai Yuan Guan," which was a well-known temple in the capital city. Startled, the old man woke up but didn't understand the meaning of this strange dream. Days later he went back to the fields and heard the same voice again. He went to the county governor and told him of his experience but the governor said that it was silly nonsense. But that same night, the dream reoccurred and he saw the same man wearing the same black clothes, who said that he had been suffering for a long time underground and that "You must move me or else there will be a disaster." So the next day, he and his sons went to the fields and began digging. There they found a bell, the same color as the clothes of the man in his dream. At daybreak, the bell started making loud sounds without being struck. The people were surprised and frightened and told the county governor, who then realized that this must be an important bell, and in turn reported the matter to the emperor Xuan Zong. Emperor Xuan Zong consulted with his prime minister Li Lin Pu, who recorded the story. The bell was moved as instructed and all agreed that whatever disaster was impending had been avoided. The bell was an obvious omen of good luck.

Bird

Dreams of birds have many meanings, both good and bad, requiring expert interpretation.

Chen Shi Yuan's book of dream interpretation tells that birds, especially the phoenix, are benevolent, while other texts see them as as malevolent in certain circumstances "If someone dreams of a bird flying into a house, it means death or evil." There are variations of this theme. Because a crow is a wild bird, a dream of a crow entering a house means that the people will abandon the house, leaving it to go wild.

A book on dreams by Zhou Xuan considers the chicken a symbol of a military official because it has a crown on its head, thus "If someone dreams of a rooster, it means that one will be an unhappy military official." The *Tai Ping Yu Lan* says, "The chicken is a symbol of a military official but the rooster is a symbol of an unhappy military official. If one dreams of a crowd of chickens entering a house, it means that the official who lives there will be arrested. If crowds of chickens are fighting inside a house, it means that there will be quarrels and fighting."

If one dreams of a peacock he or she will have literary talents or pursue a literary career, while the magpie appearing in a dream portends happiness. A different chapter of the *Tai Ping* identifies a parrot as an ill omen. "If someone dreams of a parrot, that person will die."

If someone dreams of *zhou qin,* a mythical bird, it means that he or she will remain single. If a married man dreams of it, it means that he might lose his wife. If both male and female birds appear in the same dream, it means that there is too much sexual activity in the relationship.

See also Cock (Rooster), Crane, Peacock, Phoenix, Quail

Zhu Ji Weng, an immortal associated with chickens (Wang).

Yu the Great, shooting out eight of the earth's original nine suns (Xiao).

Boat

A dream of a boat is a sign of good fortune.

Since they are used to traverse rivers, major obstacles in any long journey, boats were seen, with some exceptions, as supportive to important endeavors of life. One essay says, "The benefits of boats are just as those of horses and horse carts, as as they bring wonderful things from far away and support the universe." Interpreters considered dreams of boats, especially a boat under full sail or being aboard a moving boat, as omens of success. If a family member who has been ill has dreamed of getting off of a boat, it meant that the part of the body in which the flow of Qi was interrupted (and hence causing the illness) would become unblocked, and recovery would follow; however, a dream of a boat sinking or turning over or the passenger being covered with water was a sign of bad luck or disease.

In *The New Collection of Zhou Gong's Dream Interpretations*, there are similar interpretations: "If one dreams of falling into a boat, it is a good omen. If one dreams of a boat turning over, it means there are worries about disease and death. If one dreams of a boat full of things, it means there will be a serious disease. If one dreams of a boat going forward, it means great luck. If one dreams of a boat going slowly in the gentle wind, it is also sign of good luck. If one dreams of a sick patient getting on a boat, it predicts a fortunate recovery."

Bow and Arrow

A portent of success.

Interpreters based this interpretation on a homophone of the word for "bow," which is pronounced *gong*, the same sound as the word for "success" or "achievement." However, the opposite interpretation has also been given.

In Chen Shi Yuan's book of dream interpretation, it says that "Hun Tian had a dream and in the dream he entered into the sea with a bow. Later he achieved success in his endeavors." A variation of this story records that Hun Tian dreamed a god presented a bow to him. He then claimed a kingdom, Funan, based on the authority of this bow.

In contrast, the *New Collection of Zhou Gong's Dream Interpretations* explains, "Dreams of broken bows and arrows mean that one's plans will not succeed."

Brush (see Pen)

Cart

A dream of a cart is a sign of becoming a great official.

Carts pulled by horses for passenger use were vehicles that only the very wealthy could afford, and thus were used only by high-ranking officials. Interpreters thus associated horse carts in dreams with wealth and nobility, an explanation is repeatedly seen in dream literature. Some interpretations recorded: "Dreams of riding a cart while going to the city will bring great fortune to the dreamer" and "Dreams of moving forward while following a cart means that an official position will be in one's future."

Disabled Cart

A dream of a disabled cart is an omen of coming misfortune.

While those who could afford a cart were wealthy officials, a dream of a disabled cart, especially any damage to its wheels, was an unfavorable sign. A dreams of a cart without wheel spokes also portended failure.

Cat

A dream of a cat is a sign of impending hostilities or conflicts.

The *Chao Ye Jian Zai* tells that Xue Ji Yong, governor of the county of Ji Zhou, dreamed of a cat was lying at the door of his front hall with its face turned toward the outside. He asked the interpreter Zhang Xian about the meaning of this dream and Zhang pointed out that the cat has teeth and paws, used for hunting and protection. "If it lies at the door, it is intending to block dangers from without. It means that there must be an army coming." In less than ten days another official in Jui Zhou started a rebellion.

Clothing and Accessories

The color, quality, and condition of clothes and shoes offer important clues as to whether one's dreams portend good or evil.

Interpretations of clothing dreams are based on various lines of reasoning. For example, shoes are associated with harmony, since the word for shoe, *xie,* has the same pronunciation as a word meaning harmony. New clothes are associated with disease in view of the fact that the dead are dressed in new clothes for funerals. White clothing is associated with good fortune, based on a contradictory method of association, since white is the color for funerals. Dirty clothes are associated with an illness of one's wife, since washing clothes was regarded as the work of the wife; the same is true of torn clothing. A waist belt is associated with official rank, since a belt is indeed an accessory indicating rank; and, lastly unbuttoned clothing is associated with quarreling and fighting, as those activities would likely lead to such a state.

The *Tai Ping Yu Lan* states that "Upper garments or clothes covering the upper body are symbols of the husband. If a woman dreams of a coat or clothing covering the upper body, she will have a good husband." It also says that, "Shoes and socks are symbols of children, belonging to the body forever. If one dreams of shoes and socks, one will soon bear a child. Shoes are a symbol of the male; socks are a symbol of the female." Further, it says, "Rough shoes mean messengers, belonging to a lower class, or traveling far. A dream of obtaining rough shoes will bring one servants and messengers."

The *New Collection of Zhou Gong's Dream Interpretations* records that: "New clothes indicate disease; clothes untied or with missing buttons, quarrels; black clothes, becoming an official; yellow clothes, great fortune; green clothes, the wife being pregnant; white clothes, good fortune; red clothes, official business; women's clothing, an ill omen; putting on clothes, a good omen; broken clothes with holes, worrying about wife's becoming ill; torn wrapping cloth, an ill omen; new wrapping cloth, a good omen; new socks, good luck; worn or torn socks, bad luck; any kind of shoes, a hundred things in harmony; waist belt, a sign of official rank."

See also Silk

Clouds

Dreams of clouds portend good fortune.

Interpreters believed that dreams of colorful clouds close to the body would bring luck. Clouds further would predict the excellence of the writing and calligraphy, the most prized of the arts, of the dreamer. In *Elegant Talks in the Studio Jun Ge* is a story of the famous poet and scholar Zhang Jing, who relates that when he was young he used to work diligently to write poetry; however, in spite of his hard work, he did not succeed. One night he had a dream in which he saw five-colored cloud that came down from the sky. He plucked one piece of the cloud and swallowed it. Following this dream, he no longer had to struggle to write well and later he became a great poet.

A story of Zhang Jing in the *Tai Ping Guang Ji* relates that when he passed the civil service examination at the highest level, called *jin shi,* he went to Huai Zhou. He had a dream in which he saw a piece of lucky cloud cover his body and that year he took another examination, responding to the emperor's questions. His answers were correct and he placed first among the examinees.

On the other hand, if one dreams of a black cloud covering the sky and sun, it is an evil omen. The *Book of Sui* tells that during the reign of emperor Zhuang of the Northern Wei, Tuo Po Shun once dreamed that he saw a black cloud coming from the northwest and moving southeast. All the light from the sun, moon, and stars was blocked; all was in darkness. But soon the clouds disappeared and the sun came out again and in the southwest it became bright once again. Tuo Po Shun told his dream to an interpreter who explained it thus: "The black cloud coming from the north indicates that an enemy from the north will march on the capital. In the dream the sun was the emperor, the moon was the empress, and the stars were all his ministers. The black cloud coming meant there was impending disaster coming to the country, but since the sun came back out, all will be well once again." All of the above later transpired.

The birth of the immortal Lin Ling Su was foretold by his mother's dream of an encounter with a red cloud (Wang).

Cock (Rooster)

An omen of violence.

A dream of cock or rooster indicates quarrels and fighting, leading to violence. This is no doubt related to the fact that the rooster is seen as an aggressive bird that is used in cockfighting, particularly in southern China; the crown on its head has also made it an appropriate symbol of officials, who are seen by the general population as prone to quarrels. It is recorded in the *Tai Ping Yu Lan* that a dream of this violent animal indicates the coming of violence in one's life. However, the rooster is not all bad. The cock is the tenth sign of the zodiac. The red rooster is believed to protect against fire, while the white rooster drives off demons.

Coffin

An omen of riches.

As containers for the dead, coffins originally were symbols of bad luck. As we have seen, however, dream interpreters often consider the significance of homophones to arrive at opposite associations. Coffin in Chinese, *guan cai,* has the same pronunciation as *guan* (high official) and *cai* (treasure), so one who dreams of a coffin will achieve high rank and fortune. Interpreters also felt that the more fearful was the dream involving the coffin, the greater the luck the dreamer would have. For instance, if the dreamer saw an open coffin, a coffin with the body talking, he would have even greater fortune. One text claims, "One who dreams of entering a coffin will receive a high position together with great fortune. One who sees the wood of his coffin in a dream will be promoted, and the government's business will be successful. If one sees a dead body in a shining coffin, a fortune will be received. If one dreams that he is kowtowing toward a coffin, it is also good fortune."

Similar interpretations are recorded in the *New Collection of Zhou Gong's Dream Interpretations.* A story in *The Book of Jin* relates how a man named Chong dreamed that two coffins fell from the sky onto the ground in front of him. Suo Chen was asked to interpret this dream and said that it meant a nobleman from the capital city would recommend him to be promoted two levels. Soon afterward, Situ Wang Rong indeed recommended Chong for a position two ranks higher.

A Collection of the Unusual tells the story of Li Feng Ji, whose maid once dreamed of a man carrying a coffin into the backyard of his home. The man told her that it was to be left there for a while. She recounted her dream to Li but he was unsure of its meaning. However, soon afterward Li was promoted to the rank of education minister and later he became prime minister.

Colt (see Horse)

Combs (see Cosmetics)

Cosmetics

Cosmetics are omens of unsolved difficulties.

The appearance in dreams of women's cosmetics and objects of jewelry were considered significant. In the *Tai Ping Yu Lan,* it states that "The hairpin is a symbol of the body, a sign of self-respect. A dream of a good hairpin brings pleasure to the body" and "A dream of a comb means the release of worries. Smooth and shining hair brings a relaxed mood."

"A dream of fragrant items such as perfume brings both the wife and daughter (women) back home" while "Dreams of pins and strips of cloth are signs of worrying about being bound; pins and belts on one's body mean that the person is bound; holding pins and belts means solving problems or getting away from one's concerns."

On the other hand, interpretations of these objects were not always consistent. Other books state "Dreams of combs make hundreds of things unsuccessful. Dreams of flowers, hairpins, cosmetic powders, and the like bring gossip and quarrels." These contradictory interpretations perhaps depended upon one's sex, for if one were male, dreams about female things were considered to be reflecting a disturbance of Confucian virtues.

Comet

An omen of impending disaster.

The *Yan Zi Chun Qiu* records that the emperor Jing Gong of Qi dreamed of a comet, which the common people call a "broom star" or "ghost star." To all, however, it has the meaning of impending disaster. The emperor immediately called Yan Zi to interpret the dream. Yan Zi said that his interpretation was not as important as whether the emperor were virtuous and beloved by his subjects. If disasters were to come to the country, Yan Zi felt that they would not be from the heavens but from the emperor. The comet dream simply indicated that if the emperor lived a luxurious life and paid no heed to the needs and wishes of his subjects, they would revolt and the prediction of the "broom star" would come true.

Confucius (Kong Zi)

An omen of success.

An example of this type of dream occurred in the late Zhou dynasty. It is written that Guo Wei dreamed of Confucius. When he awoke, he felt spirited and strong, and he later won a battle against his enemy. He attributed his success to the dream of Confucius.

Cow

Dreaming of a cow can have many meanings but it most often symbolizes the family and the home.

According to five elements theory the cow has the nature of earth, and therefore the cow is also called an "earth cow." Since the earth is related to Yin, as are the dark, the mysterious, the female, etc., the cow is associated with wives or concubines, as well as with mothers, sons, and nurturing. Ancient Chinese considered the cow a beast of burden used to carry necessities and as a source of power for tilling and planting. As the main source of labor for agricultural production, it is also a symbol for food and thus household prosperity. The cow further has been associated with official rank, and scholarship. Early interpreters used these several associations when interpreting the meaning of cows in dreams.

Dreaming of a cow is generally a good omen. One text says that "If someone dreams of seeing cows and horses, it is a good omen. If someone dreams of a cow leading a man, it means everything that is pursued will be accomplished, a good omen." It goes on to state, however, that if in a dream a cow or horse is killed, it means disruption of the family and if a cow or horse is seen going out of a house, it means adultery has taken place. And a dream of killing a cow means that one's family may soon face ruin.

According to the eight diagrams, both the cow and horse belong to fire, *li*. Therefore, if someone dreams of cows or horses entering a house, it means that the house will catch fire, again, a major disruption of the home. Thus it is recorded "If one sees cows and horses inside a room in a dream, it is an ill omen."

A Bleeding Cow
An omen of promotion to a higher position.

In a story from the *Three Kingdoms* a man named Jiang Wan was a lower ranked official, a careless person whose lack of attention to detail caused him difficulties. Several times he was almost killed by the emperor Liu Bei for failing to perform up to expectations. However, the prime minister, Zhu Ge Liang, understood that Jiang Wan was a talented person and had intervened on his behalf several times. Jiang Wan reported that he had a dream which he saw a cow's head in front of a gate, with blood pouring from it. When he awoke, he was frightened as he felt that this was an inauspicious omen. He went to the well-known dream interpreter Zhao Zhi who interpreted the dream thusly: "Seeing blood is an omen that something amazing will happen. The nose and horns of the cow form the shape of the character *gong*, which also has the meaning of 'high-ranking official.' Thus the dream is a wonderful omen that means high rank will soon come to you." Soon afterward Jiang was appointed as the governor of a county and following this appointment, he was promoted by Zhu Ge Liang to the position of minister of education.

Cow with Two Tails
**A dream of a cow with two tails indicates
survival in spite of difficulty.**

The interpretation of dream of a cow with two tails provides another example of using written characters as an important analytical tool. A cow with two tails would look similar to the character *shi,* which means wrongdoing. The book *Yi Yuan* tells of the story of a businessman named Zhou Shan, who one day was traveling by boat down a river. One night he dreamed he saw a cow with two tails jumping into the water. Soon there was a severe storm and the boat began to sink. However, because Zhou Shan had been unable to sleep, thinking about what events were portended by his dream, he was able to escape. So it turned out that a cow with two tails means surviving a dangerous situation.

Crane

A dream of a crane means longevity or immortality.

The crane has traditionally symbolized longevity. It flies high in the skies above the dusty world and is thus also a symbol of cleanliness and purity. As the crane is a wild bird it is always seen to be free. The ancients considered "a crane standing among chickens" as a phrase meaning that the crane has unusual ability and is not of the common world. A dream of a flying crane is a good omen, portending that the dreamer will become a high official.

The *New Book of Tang* identifies Zhang Jiu Ling as a famous poet of the Tang dynasty. When Zhang was born, his mother dreamed that nine cranes flew from the sky and landed in the yard of their home. The boy was therefore named Jiu Ling, meaning "nine years" of age. His literary name was Zhi Shou, a person of longevity. He later passed the highest level of the civil service examinations and became prime minister.

Another story, in the *Book of Liao,* tells that when a respected official named Huan Yan Hui abandoned the Liao kingdom and headed north, the emperor had a dream in which he saw a white crane fly away from his own military camp. But it soon returned. The next morning the emperor told his ministers of this dream and said, "Huan Yan Hui must be returning." This proved later to be true.

The immortal Ding Ling Wei transformed into a crane (Wang).

The crane is also a symbol of immortality. Thus, a dream of a crane fly-ing away can also mean that death is coming. In the *Jian Wen Zalu,* it is related that during the Tang dynasty the well-known poet Ou Yang Xiu vis-ited the Jiang Shi Temple and prayed for a son. At that time his parents dreamed that a female crane flew toward them; shortly afterward, his wife gave birth to a beautiful daughter. When his daughter was eight, Ou Yang Xiu had another dream of a crane, which this time was flying away. A few days after this dream, his daughter suddenly died.

Crying

Crying in dreams is an omen of happiness.

Although crying typically accompanies sadness, ancient interpreters used contrary associations to explain the crying that occurred in dreams. The *Book of Zhuang Zi* says "Drinking wine leads one to dream of crying. The crier of the dream will lead a hunting party." Chen Shi Yuan considered these dreams as an example of "opposite dreams" and said that "When there is a wedding, marriage, or family reunion, one will dream of crying; when there are quarrels, accidents, and lawsuits, there are then dreams of dancing and singing. These are called opposite dreams." Other books reiterate that, "Seeing crying in dreams indicates abundance and happy events; seeing peo-ple walking and crying together means there will be no more ghosts around and thus is a good sign; seeing weeping is a happy thing."

Curtains

A dream of curtains is associated with feelings of security.

Curtains and screens serve a functional purpose as barriers. A screen was fre-quently placed inside the front gate of Chinese homes to keep a visitor from viewing the living area before being invited in. Therefore, curtains or screens have provided security and ensured privacy. The *Tai Ping Yu Lan* says that curtains and screens are for hiding behind, giving one a feeling of safety and security, an association that is carried through to one's dreams.

Dancing (see Singing)

Date (Jujube)

**A dream of the Chinese date (jujube) means that
one will have a great future.**

The famous scholar Zeng Zi was born to a poor and insignificant family. When asked how he became so learned and talented, he said that his mother had a dream when she was pregnant of eating a date. After he was born, his mother told him that this dream was an auspicious omen that he would become celebrated as one of the greatest students of Confucius. Her interpretation turned out to be correct.

Deer

A dream of a deer portends wealth and longevity.

The Chinese word for deer is *lu*, the same sound (but a different character) as a word meaning "treasure" or "property." Interpreters viewed deer dreams as portents of high office, great fortune, or longevity. The association with longevity derives from the Chinese use of ground horn of the deer as a medicinal ingredient to promote longevity. In the *Book of the Southern Dynasty*, it is written that a person named Ji Shi Zhan was simultaneously the governor of two counties for a lengthy period; moreover, he was known for being a good governor who never accepted a bribe. While he was not as rich as other officials, he lived a clean, simple life. Before he became governor, Ji dreamed that he received a bunch of deerskins. In his dream, he counted them and found that there were eleven skins. When he awoke he was overjoyed in remembering this dream as the felt that receiving deer meant that he was going to be come an official. As his dream foretold, he did so and for eleven terms held official positions. After he finished his eleventh term as the governor of two counties, he was saddened that his term had come to an end. Soon he became sick. He refused to see the doctor and shortly thereafter passed away.

Daoist masters Mao Bo Dao and Liu Dao Gong riding deer (Wang).

In the *Chao Ye,* there is a story of Shi Si Ming, one of a group of generals of the Tang Dynasty who betrayed the emperor and tried to overthrow him. Awakened by a dream which startled him, Shi Si Ming worried about its meaning, and told his son. He said that in his dream he saw a herd of deer standing in water. It appeared that they were on sand. In his dream he chased them but when the herd got to the bank of the river, they all died and the river dried up. After telling this dream to his son, he excused himself and went to the toilet. His servants, who knew Shi to be very cruel, were eavesdropping and having heard of his dream were overjoyed. They reasoned that as deer had the meaning of official rank and water the meaning of life, this dream of deer dying and water drying meant that Shi's life and office were coming to an end. That same night Shi's life did come to an end, as his son Chao Yi murdered him.

Dog

An omen of quarrels, fighting, and emotional disruption.

According to the eight diagrams, the dog belongs to the west and has the nature of gold and the season of autumn. Gold in its purest form is closer to white than yellow and is the symbol for weapons. Autumn on the other hand is the symbol of death and killing. Therefore, a dog appearing in a dream indicates emotional ills, fighting, and killing. Interpreters thus generally considered dog dreams to be omens of death and disasters.

Chen Shi Yuan tells that in the city of Liang Zhou there was an official named Zhang Tian Xi, who dreamed of a long, green dog that came from the south and wanted to bite him. In an effort to avoid the dog, Zhang ran into his house and hid in his bedroom. Not long after this dream, an army from the south attacked and destroyed Liang Zhou. It was led by a general wearing a long green robe by the name of Gou Chang, whose name has the same pronunciation as the words for dog (*gou*) and long (*chang*).

In folk belief, the dog is a wild animal and thus a premonition of death in the wild. If one dreamed of a dog coming into the house, it thus meant that someone would die in the fields. The *Book of the Southern Dynasty* tells a story of Zhu Zheng, a doctor for the emperor Tan Yi. Once Zhu Zheng had a dream in which he saw two animals, a dog and a sheep, sitting at the emperor's feet. He told this strange dream to others, saying dogs and sheep are not signs of good luck, and seeing them both sitting at the emperor's feet in the dream must mean that there was something wrong or something bad about to happen. Soon after, a general betrayed the emperor, rebelling and establishing his own kingdom. The general returned to attack the emperor's city, driving the emperor out into the countryside where he subsequently died.

Strangely enough, a dream of dogs fighting has been interpreted to mean that a guest will soon arrive. The *Book of Xin* also states that if someone dreams of a dog biting people, a distinguished guest will soon arrive.

A more typical dog dream is found in the book *Yue Jue Shu*, which tells that Fu Chai, king of Wu, once dreamed of seeing three black dogs barking in the south of the city while he was facing north. The dogs then went to the north of the city and began barking again. People in the area were cooking but there was no smoke rising from their kitchens. The king was perplexed by this dream, not knowing if it was a good or ill omen, and so he called upon a scholar named Sun Sheng to interpret it. When Sun Sheng heard the dream he bid farewell to his wife, saying that this evil dream would bring disaster but that it was his duty to tell the truth, even if he incurred the king's wrath. He told the king that this dream meant that he would be overthrown, for a dog barking means that a temple is without a monk and cooking without smoke means that there is no food to eat. When the king heard this interpretation, he became angry and had Sun Sheng executed. Gou Jian, the leader of the Yue people to the north soon descended upon Wu, killing Fu Chai.

Puppy
Portends becoming pregnant by a spirit and bearing a son with great filial piety.

The *Book of the Southern Dynasty* tells that Zhang Jing Er's mother fell asleep in the fields and dreamed that a puppy with horns was licking her. She later became pregnant and gave birth to a son whom she named Doggy, and some time later had another boy whom she named Piggy. Both sons grew up to be great officials.

The eldest, Zhang Jing Er also became famous for making up children's songs, one of which included the line, "Who is the heaven's son? Either the dog or the pig." Children everywhere learned this song and sang it all day long. Zhang eventually worked for the emperor Ming Di who thought his

曹仙媼

The immortal Cai Xian Wen traveling with his servant and dog (Wang).

name was so vulgar that he changed it to Jing Er, meaning "Respectful son," and changed his brother's name to Mu Er, meaning "Admiring son."

White Dog
An omen of coming death.

White in China is the color of death. A story in the *Book of Jin* tells of Wang Dun having a dream in which he saw a white dog coming down from the sky to bite him. He saw knives and a cart, with people on the left and people on the right. Perplexed by the dream, he didn't know if he should be frightened or not. But soon after the dream Wang died at the age of fifty-nine.

Doors

An omen of descendants who are doomed to failure.

A dream of doors means that one's offspring or grandchildren will be unsuccessful in their business or careers. It is recorded that this omen stems from the belief that male children are responsible for not only continuing the name of one's family but "enlarging the doors and gates of the family's property," a traditional metaphor for prosperity. A dream of doors indicates one's concern about being unsuccessful, which surely follow.

Dragon

An omen of coming good fortune.

The ancient Chinese believed that the dragon had special powers. It was born in the deep sea and had the ability to travel by swimming or flying through the sky while leaving no evidence of a trail. In contrast to the dragons of the West, which were believed to be an evil beasts, the Chinese dragons were thought to have purely positive qualities. It was believed that this animal controlled the rains that nourished crops. Possessing the essence of the nature of insects, the dragon could be tiny or huge, short or long, could fly high in the sky or low to the earth, and could be bright or dark or visible or invisible at will. The book *Hong Fan* ascribes to the dragon the nature of

Yang and considers it a noble animal demanding respect. It further notes that dream interpreters saw the dragon as a symbol of the emperor.

The Book of the Southern Dynasty relates that the emperor Qi Gao, called Xiao Dao in his youth, at age seventeen had a dream of riding on the back of a black dragon chasing the sun in the western sky. When the sun was almost behind the mountain, the dragon stopped. Xiao Dao awakened in great fear of the meaning of his dream. His parents took him to a dream interpreter who to his surprise told him that this dream was an omen of nobility. The sunset, the sun falling behind the mountain, meant that the fortune of the Song dynasty was declining and to his good fortune, his own dynasty could then be established. Soon after, the Song dynasty was indeed overthrown and Xiao Dao became the first emperor of the ensuing dynasty.

Another text tells of emperor Li Sheng of the Southern Tang dynasty, who during a daytime nap had a dream in which he saw a yellow dragon. The dragon surrounded the gate of the palace and its fishlike skin reflected a light that covered the whole palace. After he awoke, he asked someone to check the front gate of the palace, where his son was found about to enter to visit his father. Interrogating his son about what time he had arrived and the position in which he was standing at the gate, and so on, he found that every fact coincided with what he had dreamed. Li Sheng believed that this was no mere coincidence but an omen from the heavens. He thenceforth proclaimed this son as his successor.

A dream of seeing a dragon without a tail or feet or a dragon falling to the ground portends the end of the state or the dynasty. The *Gu Jin Tu Shu* tells that when emperor Yang of the Sui dynasty, Yang Guang, was born, the whole sky was filled with red light. Cows and horses were mooing and whinnying, and his mother dreamed that a dragon came out of her body, flew high into the sky and then fell to the ground, breaking its tail. The wife, thinking this an odd dream, told her husband, emperor Wen Di, who said nothing. Fearing that this dream carried an ill omen, he made an effort to change the fortune of the son, paying special attention to him and showering him with love. Still, whenever he saw this son he felt unhappy. When his son finally came to power as emperor, he led the country to war. These decisions ultimately destroyed the kingdom of Sui.

A dragon dream is also sometimes taken to mean that the dreamer will get to see the emperor. Liu Bang, the first emperor of the Han dynasty, took Bo Ji as his concubine. Bo Ji was at the court for over a year but never had a chance to be intimate with the emperor. One night she dreamed she saw a

The birth of China's greatest poet, Li Bai, was foretold by his mother's dream of her future son riding a red dragon (Wang).

huge dragon resting on her stomach. The following day the emperor summoned her. When she told the emperor of her dream he said that the dream was indicative of noble future for her. Later she gave birth to his son who was to become emperor Hui. She was subsequently titled Tai Hou, mother of the emperor.

In another story that took place in the Five Dynasties period, a monk built a temple along the road and grew vegetables to support himself. One day he took a nap and dreamed that he saw a golden dragon eating his vegetables. After waking he thought that this must be an omen that someone important was coming to see him. He then saw a huge man eating vegetables exactly as he had seen the dragon doing in his dream. The monk stared for a long time at this man, who looked strangely handsome, powerful and yet severe. The monk gave the man food and told him of his dream. They talked for awhile and then swore that no matter what fortune befell them, they would not forget one another. The large man later became the first emperor of the Song dynasty, Zhao Quang Yin. After he came to power, he sought the monk and found him. A huge temple was built to which was given the name Pu An Du, or Place of Peace.

Dragon Carrying Someone to the Roof
A symbol of impending death.

The *Book of Jin* tells a story about a man named Guo Yu, who was a devout Daoist. He became involved in a rebellion but was defeated. While the emperor sought him to put him to death, he had a dream in which he was riding a black dragon into the sky. However, the dragon alighted on the roof and stopped. When he awoke this dream caused him great concern. The dragon should have flown into the sky, but in his dream the dragon instead stopped at the rooftop. Because the house was a place where a dead body should remain, he felt this dream to be a symbol of impending death and so arranged his own funeral. Soon afterward he died, proving his dream true.

Dragon Flying into Someone's Chest
An omen of accomplishing something important.

In the *Xi Jing Za Ji* is a story of a prime minister of the Han dynasty, Dong Zhong Shu, dreaming of a dragon flying into his chest. Following this dream he was inspired to write a book called *Chun Qiu Fan Lu,* a treatise of the book *Chun Qiu,* which was supposed to have been written by Confucius. This very important book expounds on the concept of Yin and Yang as well as the five elements. Dong Zhong Shu was hence known to be a key scholar in the development of Confucianism in the Han dynasty.

See also Snake

Earth

A symbol of loyalty and stability.

Earth is viewed as the mother of all things, while the sky is seen as the father. The nature of earth is Yin (dark, passive, female) and it is one of the five elements as well. In the eight diagrams, earth belongs to *kun,* and its direction is the center. When the earth is related to human beings it refers to looking, talking, seeing, hearing, and thinking, activities which it governs. Of the five virtues, it is related to loyalty. At the imperial court, it is related to the internal court (residence of the empress). These basic principles were used by interpreters to interpret dreams about earth.

Since earth is related to Yin and mother, dreams about the crumbling or breaking earth have the meaning that a mother is filled with worry. Since earth is the combination of all Qi and heavenly things, dreams about earth also indicate stability in health. If one dreams that he is falling onto the earth, it means that he will lose his position. And, since people are buried in the earth after death, dreams of being covered by the earth are indeed portents of evil.

According to *The New Collection of Zhou Gong's Dream Interpretations,* earth is the source of all things, and thus a symbol of richness and high rank. Therefore, seeing the earth, lying on the earth, being on the earth, entering into the earth, even experiencing light coming out of the earth all have auspicious meanings. On the other hand, sweeping the earth or seeing dirty earth on clothes is bad luck. Since earth is the foundation of a house, a dream of the earth sinking means there will be trouble concerning one's home. A dream of the earth moving means that one will be moving in the near future.

The Remaining Books of Dunhuang state that "Dreaming of buying land is an extremely lucky omen." *The Copied Books in the Bei Tang Studio* says, "Dreaming of seeing the earth means one is at peace and in good health."

The *Tai Ping Guang Ji* records a story that before the ruler Fu Jian was thinking of invading the south, he dreamed one night that the whole city grew vegetables and the earth was becoming unbalanced, i.e., becoming skewed to the southeast. The court interpreter said that an overabundance of vegetables meant difficulty in becoming a general, while the earth sinking in the southeast meant that it would be difficult to maintain peace on that side of the river.

Eating

Eating a Bird's Egg
An omen of finding one's talents.

The *Tai Ping Yu Lan* states that Luo Jun Zhang at age twenty had little ambition, either in studies or finding a profession that interested him. In fact, he was quite lazy and slept most of the day. One day he had a dream in which he found a bird egg of five colors. He did not feel that this egg was from this world and ate it. He later awakened from a deep sleep and felt that he had undergone some change. From that day onward, he became very diligent in his studies, which led him to great literary success.

Eating Cherries
A symbol of imagined good luck.

You Yang Za Zu tells of a man who fell in love with a neighborhood girl. One night the man dreamed of eating a cherry thrown out by the girl. After the dream, he woke up to find a cherry pit next to his pillow. Although he found the cherry pit and remembered the dream, he wondered: Did he actually eat the cherry? Or was it all in his imagination? A dream of eating cherries is thus a pleasant dream, but only an act of the imagination.

Eating Lamb
A dream of eating lamb is an omen of a wish coming true.

Prime minister Zhung Qi Xian got drunk one day and rested on a large rock and fell asleep. He dreamed he saw a flock of sheep being driven in front of him, and heard a voice telling him "Please eat the meat of sheep."

However, after eating many pounds of lamb meat, he grew weary of eating and after waking up, although he remembered the dream, he was confused by its meaning. But he grew to be very skilled at raising sheep, which before his dream he knew nothing about.

Eating Melon
A dream of eating melon is a wish for immortality.

The *Shi Yi Ji* tells that the mother of emperor Ming of the Han dynasty had a dream of eating a strange melon. She felt this to be an auspicious dream and sent messengers everywhere to look for this most unusual fruit. At long last, messengers found a huge, delicious peach-shaped melon over three feet long. They told her that this melon was from the land of the immortals and after eating it she would live to be ten thousand years old. However, after the empress ate the melon, she died and her servants found melon seeds and bits of the core of the fruit within her wounds. Obviously the melon did not confer longevity, so it was concluded that a dream of eating melon was merely a wish for immortality.

Eating a Pearl
An omen of death.

Since pearls and jade are signs of nobility, a pearl or piece of jade was often placed in the mouth of a deceased family member. Related to this ritual, a dream of eating a pearl or piece of jade was considered an omen of death. *The Book of Zuo* tells the story of Sheng Bo, who dreamed that he crossed a river, where someone brought pearls to him and asked him to eat them. Sheng Bo cried and his tears turned to pearls covering his chest. He then sang a song saying, "Across the river I was given the pearls. Returning, returning, the pearls are all on my chest." After he awoke, he was so frightened of this portent of death that he did not dare to consult a dream interpreter, nor did he have the courage to tell anyone about it. As time passed, however, he felt less and less afraid of the dream. Three years later, as he was leading an army into battle, he had completely gotten over it. Moreover, with large army under his command, what did he have to fear? He then told others about his dream and how it had turned out to mean nothing. But, as fate would have it, that same day Sheng Bo was killed in battle.

Eating Sesame Paste or Porridge
A portent of of success at fulfilling the needs of one's child.

In the *Book of Southern Qi* is a story of the empress Qi, who gave birth to the next emperor. When the Emperor was two months old, she lacked breast milk and was unable to provide the nourishment that the child needed. She dreamed one night that she was given two bowls of sesame porridge, which she ate. When she awakened she felt fullness in her breast and to her astonishment found that her breast milk was plentiful.

Egg

A symbol of future talent and increased knowledge.

Eggs are seen as nourishment for the body and, being round, they have a symbolic meaning of continuity and eternity. But in interpreting dreams, eggs were seen as providing nourishment to one's literary skills. Liu Ke of the Tang dynasty once dreamed of eating chicken eggs and he later became an expert in the Confucian classics. He also won fame as a great scholar.

See also Eating a Bird's Egg

Elephant

A portent of gaining a position of power.

The elephant, once indigenous to China and an animal revered in Buddhism, was believed to be the largest of beasts and thus was a symbol of strength and power, and by extension a guard or keeper of important or valuable property. Interpreters believed that one who dreamed of an elephant would become governor of a city or even ruler of a country. But a contrary omen related to the tusks of the elephant, which were made of valuable ivory, utilized for offerings for the gods and a material for fashioning ornaments as well as drinking and eating utensils for the wealthy. Since the elephant's ivory tusks could be the cause of their demise, a dream of elephants also carried the meaning of impending disaster.

The *Zuo Zhuan* remarks that elephants have tusks that bring disaster to themselves and that a dream of tusks symbolizes surrendering to overpowering forces or doing evil deeds. Taking these associations together, some interpreters considered elephant dreams as not only portents that the dreamers would become high officials but also that they would die in office because of some strange disaster. The *Book of Jin* tells of Zhang Mao, a young man who dreamed of an elephant. The interpreter Wan Tui said that Zhang would become the governor of a county but would not die of natural causes. Zhang indeed did become a governor and but later there was an uprising in which he, three of his sons, and his brother were all killed.

Facial Features

Changing One's Face
An omen of a change in one's luck.

In these dreams, one's face or appearance has changed. Interpreters considered this type of dream as a sign of luck changing either to good or bad. In the *Meng Zhan Yi Zhi* is a story about Li Sheng Mei, a county governor in the Tang dynasty who one day dreamed that his own head turned into that of a tiger. When he awoke he worried that this dream was not one of good luck. That night his wife dreamed that she looked into a mirror and saw the reflection not of her own head but also that of a tiger. But when she awoke, she was very happy, reasoning that since the emperor is seen as a dragon and ministers are seen as tigers, this dream was an omen of new appointment. Ten days later the emperor indeed called on Li and promoted him to prime minister. Coinciding with his appointment, his wife was also given a high title.

The story of Zhou Bi Da is recorded in *The Book of Songs*. It tells that Zhou felt very unsuccessful in his career but one night dreamed he overheard people talking in the hall, saying that his appearance was so ugly that he would never be given a good title. These people felt that his face must surly have to be changed in order for him to be favored by the emperor. After the dream, he felt an irritation on his chin that caused him to scratch. When he looked into a mirror he discovered that he now had a very attractive mustache and beard. Later, he became a prime minister.

In *The Collection of the Unusual* is the story of Tao Gu, who when young dreamed he saw a person come to him with a "heavenly edict" to change his eyes. The person was a lower-rank official who told him that if Tao Gu would give him some money he would not change his eyes. But Tao Gu would not pay a bribe and insisted that he do as he was ordered to do and leave. The official changed Tao Gu's eyes with "third-class" (not of good quality) eyes. When Tao Gu awoke from his dream he was deeply disturbed and saw his eyes had turned dark green. A fortune-teller later told him that he did not see great fortune in Tao Gu's future as "although his face was the face of a nobleman, his eyes were the eyes of a ghost."

These face-changing dreams indicate how the earlier generations perceived the relationship between appearance and riches or nobility. In *On the Eternal*, it states, "For those who can tell the future of a person, they must observe the features of the bones to prove their predictions of riches or poverty. Seeing the bones and appearances is like seeing utensils; you see them and you know what they are for."

Feces or Excrement

An omen of fortune or failure.

Dreams of feces or excrement are a sign of being unclean. *On Human Potentials*, by Wang Fu, says that "Dreams about anything dirty, foul smelling, or decaying have the meaning of something evil and are a bad omen." However, in reviewing the literature there are two ways of interpreting this type of dream that might seem contradictory. Some interpreters considered all of these dreams as ill omens while others considered them good omens.

In *The Remaining Books of Dunhuang*, it says "Seeing muddy and dirty clothes in dreams is a sign of shame." In *The New Collection of Zhou Gong's Dream Interpretations*, it says "Seeing feces and dirty clothes in dreams is a great ill omen. Dreaming of falling into a toilet indicates the dreamer will succumb to a serious disease." Nevertheless, both texts have passages interpreting these same dreams as portents of money or treasure. *The Remaining Books of Dunhuang* also says "Dreaming of seeing clothes on which there is dirt or feces is a lucky sign; so is seeing a toilet or falling into a toilet. These dreams will bring riches to the dreamer." *The New Collection of Zhou Gong's Dream Interpretations* states that "Dreams of clothes dirtied by feces or urine are a good omen, and if one dreams of seeing feces or urine on the road, he will obtain great wealth." These two ways of interpreting gave the interpreter flexibility when interpreting dreams of this type, depending upon the situation. Scholars have reasoned that the different interpretations derive from the fact that peasants associated feces, used as fertilizer and thus food for the earth, with potential good harvests, while those who did not till the fields as merely a sign of waste, a sign of bad luck.

The Book of Jin says "Hao once was asked, 'if one is to be promoted in rank, he would dream of a coffin; if one is to get money he would dream of feces. Why is that?' Hao responded, 'Guan (official rank) is originally foul smelling and decayed. So when one is going to be promoted, he will dream of a dead body. Money is originally from feces and dirt. So if one is going to receive money he will dream of those things.'"

Fire

A symbol of uncontrolled emotions.

Fire was considered the very essence of Yang Qi (the air of Yang). According to the eight diagrams of the *Book of Changes,* fire is *li,* and its direction is the south. Among the five human functions, it governs speech. Of emotions it relates to anger. Of the five organs of the body, it regulates the heart. In human affairs, it refers to the emperor. Among official positions, it indicates the prime minister.

In *On the Eternal* it is written that "A dream of fire indicates something is related to the mouth and the tongue, referring to quarrels." A further explanation of this principle in one of the earliest books on Chinese medicine states that "When the Yang air in a person's body is too strong, one dreams of fire or being burned. When the anger stays in the heart, one dreams of fire or smoke in the mountains." In another chapter of the same book, it says "If the heart Qi is too weak, one will dream of tending a fire; when the Qi is strong, one will dream of being burned."

Fire is bright and gives light, so a large fire is also a sign of prosperity. If one dreams of fire or holding fire while walking, it means good luck. If one dreams that a fire burns down one's house, it means brightness, but it also indicates bad luck. Fire is born out of wood; therefore if one dreams of taking the wood out of a fire, it indicates evil and is a negative omen.

The immortal Yao Guang, reading comfortably in the midst of a blazing fire (Wang).

The New Collection of Zhou Gong's Dream Interpretations also says that "If one dreams of pulling wood out of a fire, it is a grave evil sign." It adds, "If one dreams of seeing fire burning, it means good luck; if one dreams of holding fire [a torch] while moving quickly, it means good connections; if one dreams of a fire burning down the house, it means the parents are ill or sick."

Fist

A portent that one will become a ruler.

In the *Records of the Unique and the Strange* is recorded the story of Wen Di, who before becoming emperor was traveling on a lake in a boat. As night fell, he drifted off to sleep and had a dream in which he was astonished to find that he had lost his left hand. When he awoke he thought that this dream of losing a limb was an omen of bad luck so he went ashore and walked to a hut where an old monk lived. He described the dream to the monk and to the surprise of Wen Di, the monk rose to congratulate him. The monk said to him "This is a very fortunate dream. Without the left hand you have only a single fist, and if you can control everything under the heavens with but one hand, it means that you will become emperor." When Wen Di became emperor he never forgot this dream and its interpretation and in honor of the event he renamed the little hut Ji Xiang Shi, "Good Fortune Temple."

Fly

**Since dirt attracts flies, they are synonymous
with decaying and death.**

The fly is a symbol of filth and dirt. An ode in the *Book of Songs* tells of a black fly that boasts of being nasty and mean and spreading gossip. Flies were thought able to turn from white to black or black to white; they could even cause betrayal or uprisings. Interpreters believed that dreams of flies indicated that someone would be convinced by an evil person to act against what is good. The *Book of Han* tells that after Liu He became emperor, he dreamed he saw black flies on a mound of feces on the west stairway of the palace. The mound was so large that it appeared to be a small mountain. The interpreter Gong Sui interpreted the dream according to the *Book of Songs* saying, "Emperor, you have so many people around you that are like black flies. They are evil people and they persuade you with their evil ideas. Now you must use the intelligent and good ministers of your father's court. If you don't do this, disaster will happen." But Liu He did not heed this omen and soon was overthrown.

Because flies gather over decaying matter such as the dead, they are associated with the custom for a dead person's body to be protected for three days before burial, a rite called *hu san*, meaning "to protect the body." In order to protect the body, one had to get rid of the flies. Therefore someone dreaming of flies gathering on someone meant that he would die soon.

The history of the *The Three Kingdoms* tells a story of a wicked minister named He Yan, who continuously dreamed of seeing swarms of black flies that sometimes got in his nose. He asked the interpreter Guan Luo about this dream, and was told, "Black flies swarming on a body means that one's high official rank would be terminated. Someone holding a medium rank will die." Guan Luo told He Yan not to enjoy too much luxury but to do good and thus turn disaster into happiness. But He Yan did not listen. He continued his wicked behavior and was soon killed.

Flower

Symbols of color, brightness, beauty, women, and knowledge.

Early interpreters considered flower dreams as portents of beautiful wives and concubines. A well-known saying states that when a female is extremely beautiful, even flowers shy away from her and the moon hides itself. The flower later came to symbolize literary talents.

The Book of Songs tells that "Wu Jin, the father of Empress Wu, dreamed of going to the Shi Kang Ting [Pavilion Providing Health], where a [Chinese herbaceous] peony grew, a flower that was extremely beautiful. Under the flower Wu Jin noticed that there was a white sheep. Waking up, he felt both surprised and strange. When his daughter was born, red light covered the whole room and shone out of the windows. When she was fourteen years old, she was selected as a concubine and entered the court, later becoming the mother of an emperor."

The *Records of the Unique and the Strange* says that in the Later Han dynasty, a person named Ma Rong studied hard and had great talents. One day he dreamed he went to a beautiful flower garden where he picked several flowers and ate them. After the dream, he found there were no classical texts beyond his knowledge, and he was afterwards give the nickname Xiu Nang, "Embroidered Bag."

Another interpretation of flower dreams is that "Dreams of seeing flowers in blossom mean the dreamer has great fortune." On the other hand dreams of seeing flowers withering had the interpretation that the dreamer's wife would fall into great distress.

Food

See Eating, Grain, Fruit, Date, Peach, Melon, Pig

Grain

A dream of grain foretells of riches and good luck.

Rice, wheat, corn, and millet are all consider *fan*, an important part of the diet in China. The Chinese make a distinction between *fan* and *cai*, although both are food substances; *fan* is seen as a subsistence grain, while *cai* are those dishes eaten to give flavor to the the primary grain. A common greeting in Chinese may be translated, "Have you had your grain today?" The ancients considered grain equal to money or treasure, for without such a substance there would be no life. Interpreters thus generally considered dreams of grain as predictors of fortune.

The *Tai Ping Yu Lan* says that "Grain is food and treasure, therefore, one who dreams of grain will obtain treasure and good luck. If one dreams of grain entering one's house, prosperity will also be there." Such dreams were similarly interpreted elsewhere: "Dreams of getting grain in the marketplace is a good omen; dreams of seeing crops bring longevity; dreams of hemp, wheat, and beans indicate a feast of drinking and eating; dreams of rice and flour bring up worries about health." The latter interpretation was perhaps made because rice and flour are white, the color both of funerals and pale, unhealthy faces.

The *Book of the Later Han* tells the story of Cai Mao, a county governor in Guang Han who dreamed he was sitting in a large palace hall. Looking up to the beams on the roof, he noticed that there were three strands of wheat hanging from one beam. Cai jumped and grabbed at them, but as soon as he had the kernels in his hands, they disappeared and he was puzzled as to where they went. When he awoke he summoned the official dream interpreter Guo He, who stated, "The palace symbolizes an official place. The strands of wheat hanging from the beam mean that all of the officials have high income, and receive much compensation. When you jumped and grabbed at it, it meant that you will be promoted to one of three higher positions that will need to be filled." After a month or so, Cai Mao was indeed named to a higher rank.

Fruit

Fruits are symbols of offspring; the seeds of the fruit are likened to the bearing of many children.

The Chinese "The child has dropped" means that the child has entered the birth canal; a baby being born was imagined to be not unlike a ripe fruit falling from a tree. Fruits and their seeds have long been symbols of fertility in Chinese design, one of the most popular being that of the pomegranate. Interpreters took dreams of fruit and seeds as omens of future offspring. "If someone dreams of various fruits, it means that she will be pregnant."

Chen Shi Yuan tells that before Zhang Kong Sun was born, his father dreamed of worshipping at the Confucian Temple. In the temple he was blessed with gifts of fruit. After his dream, his wife gave birth to a son, the greatest treasure for a Chinese father.

Another story records that Shao Kang Jie's mother was ill and went to see a doctor for medicine. During her illness she dreamed of sitting at the hall door. To her left and right sides were two Chinese flowering quinces. The plant to the right side was withered and dying and her husband used medicine in an attempt to revive it, with no success. The dream was a great puzzle to her until later, when she gave birth to one boy and one girl. The boy lived and was named Shao Kang Jie, but the girl was stillborn.

See also Date, Peach, Eating Melon

Hair

Long Eyebrows
An omen of good luck portending the acquisition of power.

The Grand History tells that the emperor Shun had a dream in which he saw in a mirror that he had very long white, eyebrow hairs. His father, emperor Yao, knowing nothing about this dream, issued an edict requesting that he become the next emperor. So this type of dream became known as an omen of good luck and obtaining power.

Borrowing a Wig
An portent of baldness.

Borrowing hair or a wig foretells that one will lose one's hair. In the *Chong Ming Man Lu*, Cai Heng Zi tells a story of Jing Ji Pu, who dreamed he saw a monk coming to him and asking him to borrow his hair. The next day, he told this dream to others and in less than a month, all of his hair fell out, leaving him completely bald.

Hair Growing on the Tongue
A prediction of continuing in an official job.

This strange dream tells one that he will continue in an enviable position. The *Qing Xiang Za Ji* tells that in the Song dynasty, Ma Liang had a dream in which he saw hair growing out of his tongue. He was particularly disturbed because he didn't know if it meant that something evil would follow. An interpreter explained that if hair grew from one's tongue and one wasn't able to cut it, it meant that his official position would continue. This fortunate situation came to be true and Ma Liang told everyone its meaning.

Hand (see Fist)
Head (see Beheading)
Heart (see Organs)

Hedgehog

A hedgehog is a symbol of the destruction of one's empire.

The *Book of the Northern Dynasty* records that emperor Wu Cheng dreamed that a big hedgehog attacked his city, Ye. When he awoke, he ordered that all of the hedgehogs within the boundaries of the city be killed. People thus always associated him with the killing of these animals. When he became unpopular with his subjects because of his selfishness, they called him a hedgehog and the hedgehog became a symbol of destroying an empire.

Height

A dream of tall people portends the birth of a great man.

Great height is seen as a special attribute. Wang Fu of the later Han dynasty records in *On Human Potentials* that prior to the birth of Wen Wang, his mother had a strange dream of people who were extremely tall. Following this dream, she knew that she was going to give birth to a special son. Wen Wang later became an emperor of the Zhou dynasty.

Horns

A dream of horns growing from ones head portends evil.

The History of the Three Kingdoms tells of prime minister Zhu Ge Liang of the kingdom of Shu, who sent an army under the command of General Wei Yan to the North Valley. Wei Yan had a dream one night of horns growing out of his head. Not understanding its meaning, he went to the very famous dream interpreter Zhao Zhi. After hearing his dream, Zhao Zhi hesitated to tell him the truth and instead he said, "A Qilin [mythical beast] has but one horn and it is useless. This dream means that you will not have to fight and the enemy will destroy themselves. You will be victorious without fighting." But Zhao Zhi told other people at a later time the true interpretation, that the character for "horn," *jiao*, is a combination of

The medical specialist Ma Shi Huang treating a horse (Wang).

the words for "knife," *dao,* and "use," *yong,* and thus it is a very bad omen. In the autumn of that year, Zhu Ge Liang had Wei Yan killed with a knife because he was arrogant and refused to obey orders.

Horse

The horse has the meaning of a journey, visit, or message.

According to five elements theory, the horse belongs to Yang and has the nature of fire. It is also one of the treasures of Buddhism. In the eight diagrams it belongs to fire, *li,* and heaven, *tian.* In addition to meaning "heaven," *tian* is the symbol for empire. The text *Hong Fan* states that the horse is the fastest animal and has the nature of being royal and noble. With these characteristics it is synonymous with the emperor. In an ancient system of pronunciation, the word for horse sounded similar to *wu,* meaning military. Therefore, the horse is a also symbol for fighting and victory.

Interpreters believed that horse dreams were positive omens, for where horses were there would be victories. The *Luo Zhong Ji* tells how the first emperor of the Tang dynasty, Li Yuan, began his ascent to power following a dream in which he was wearing armor and riding several horses, while many other horses were flying through the sky. He asked aloud which army these magnificent animals belonged to and was told "The first emperor himself, who controls the whole universe." After the same dream repeated itself for several days, Li Yuan called his sons and told them that this dream was an omen that their campaign would succeed. The fighting continued until Li Yuan finally did control his universe by establishing the Tang dynasty.

Other meanings of horse dreams are a long journey, an omen of visiting friends, or sending or receiving messages. However, other texts state that if someone dreams of seeing horses and cows in the stable, it is not a good omen but a bad one.

Colt

A baby horse (colt) or donkey is a sign of impending death.

During the Tang dynasty the well-known poet Du Mu dreamed he was writing his own epitaph. When he was cooking his evening meal, the cooking pot broke. In the dream he also saw a white colt in an empty valley.

After waking, he calculated his age and realized that it was time for him to die. Soon he became very sick and not long afterward died at the age of fifty. He left a collection of his writings in twenty volumes that are still famous.

Horse Dancing in a House
An omen that foretells of the burning of one's house.

According to the eight diagrams, the horse has the nature of fire; therefore, the image of a horse dancing in a house means that the house will burn. *The Book of Jin* tells that Huang Ping once told the dream interpreter Suo Chen, "I dreamed I saw a horse dancing in a house and dozens of people clapped their hands facing the horse. What does it mean?" Suo Chen replied "Horse means fire, the dancing means fire burning, while the clapping hands facing the horse means that people come to extinguish the fire." Before Huang Ping even returned to his home, it was engulfed in flames.

Horse cart (see Cart)

House

**A portent of a gathering of family members;
a symbol of wealth and status, protection from the elements,
and security from one's enemies.**

A newly built house is a symbol of family prosperity. *The New Collection of Zhou Gong's Dream Interpretations* and *The Remaining Books of Dunhuang*, both interpret a dream of a newly built house or a house being built as an omen of great fortune. Moreover, if one watches in his dream the house being built, the dream carries a prediction of longevity. A dream of an old, broken down house, conversely, is an omen of bad luck. The first text records "If one sees in his dream a broken house, it is a evil; if one sees a fallen house, it means disease; if one sees the beams of the house are broken, it means the family is broken; if one sees an empty house, that is bad luck. If one sees in his dream that a house is leaking, it is an omen that soldiers will be defeated and people will die. If one dreams the hall of the house is sinking or falling, it means that one's official position will be lost."

The immortal Kuang Yu in his mountain hut (Wang).

If one's dream is not a dream of good luck, the bad luck falls upon the owner of the house, parents, or grandparents. The same book states that "If one sees the house moving, it means disaster for the parents. If one sees the house burning, it means that illness will come to one's parents. And as brightness is a symbol of newness and water a source of good, if one dreams of brightness in the house or sees water coming into the house, it is a symbol of great fortune and luck."

An animal in a dream appearing within the house is another matter. While cattle are said to belong in the fields and are beasts of burden, man and animals are clearly distinguished in terms of their positions and relations. Therefore if in a dream animals enter the rooms of the house it is an ill omen that symbolizes that someone in the house will die. One text states, "Seeing a cow or horse in the house is an ill omen." Because cows and horses work in the field, their entering into the house means they would plow the house into a flat field. As mentioned earlier, the horse, according to the eight diagrams, is related to *li,* fire. Therefore, a dream of a horse entering into a house carries the meaning of bringing fire to the house.

A Destroyed House
An omen that death will come to the dreamer.

A destroyed house is an omen of death, for if one's house destroyed, one's security is destroyed. This interpretation is based on a story in the *Book of Jin* about a man named Zhang Hua, who had a dream in which he saw that the emperor was in danger of being overthrown. He tried to defend the emperor but later saw that many of the houses in the area were destroyed. He awoke and shortly afterward suddenly died at age sixty-nine.

Ice

**A warning to heed the relationship
between male and female, and the time between life and death.**

The relationship between a man and a woman as well as the time between living and dying are crucial, and a dream of ice is a warning about these. *The Book of Jin* tells of a person named Hu Ce, who dreamed that he was standing on ice and was talking with a person underneath the ice. Dream interpreter

Suo Chen reasoned that above the ice was Yang while below the ice was Yin. The dream's meaning, therefore, concerned relations between male and female, or the marriage of a man and a woman. The ice is seen as a dividing line between Yang and Yin, not only the male and female, but also the living and the dead. A verse in *The Book of Songs* says, "The soldier returns for marriage, but has to await for the ice to melt." Even today in Chinese folklore, ice connotes a matchmaker or go-between in an impending marriage.

Incense Burner

A sign of pregnancy, and thus joy.

Bearing children is important for carrying on the lineage and family heritage. The first sign of pregnancy is a joyous occasion, and dreaming of an incense burner was a portent of this. A story in *Tao Hong Jing* tells that the mother of the noted scholar Jing Shi had a dream of seeing an incense burner. The day after her dream she felt that she was pregnant, which turned out to be true, and later gave birth to Jing Shi.

Ink

A dream of ink is an omen that literary skills will come in the dreamer's future.

Ink is one of the "four treasures" of the Chinese scholar and a dream of it is a positive omen. The *Draft of the History of Ming* by You Tong tells of the famous Ming dynasty painter Tang Yin, who once dreamed of being given ink by an immortal being. Following this dream, his literary skills were greatly enhanced, as were his imagination and painting skills. He became, in fact, one of China's greatest painters, and his finest works are immeasurably enhanced by his poetry and calligraphic skills.

A dream of an ink-cake in the shape of a ball is also a symbol of literary talent and skill. The *You Yang Za Zu* tells that the famous poet Wang Bo had a dream that he was given a piece of round ink. Following this dream, he no longer struggled to produce literary works, as they flowed freely. He told others of this dream and the ink ball became a symbol of literary skill.

Intestines (See Organs)

Jade

Jade is a symbol of purity, nobility, and protection from evil.

Jade has long been prized by the Chinese as a stone possessing special powers. Travelers carried pieces of jade to protect them from dangers on the road; the custom is followed to this day. Jade is also a symbol of purity and virtue; the Heavenly Emperor, lord of all gods, is also called the Jade Emperor. Interpreters believed that dreams of seeing jade, jewelry, and pearls were portents of good luck. Such dreams can also be omens of pregnancy, and hint that a person beautiful, scholarly, or noble will be born.

Insects (see Bee, Fly)

Intercourse

A symbol of imbalance of Yin and Yang, hence, disease.

A dream of sexual intercourse was considered to be the result of an imbalance of Yin Qi and Yang Qi. Such an imbalance is not a favorable sign and portends the onset of illness. A barely recognizable face appearing in this kind of dream is considered to be a "ghost," and the dream is "ghost intercourse." This imbalance and reasons for it is recorded in many medical texts, for example, in Chao Yuan Fang's *Zhu Bing Yuan Hou Zong Lun*.

Having Sex in Dream and Giving Birth to a Son
Indicative of having extramarital affairs.

Dreams indicative or extramarital affairs by either party in a marriage are unfavorable signs. The *Kai Yuan Tian Bao Yi Shi* by Wang Ren Yu of the Five Dynasties period tells of a story of Yang Guo Zhong, who later became prime minister in the Tang dynasty. In the course of his duties, he was sent to the south. His wife missed him so much that one night she had a dream in which she and her husband had intercourse and she became pregnant and gave birth to a son. When her husband returned from the south, she told him of the dream and the husband remarked that this would come true, as they loved each other so. She had, in fact, had an extramarital affair. This story became a joke of the time.

Jewelry (see Cosmetics, Jade, Pearl)

Knife

Portends coming profit or benefit.

Although it is a weapon or a utensil that might be used to injure someone, a knife is a positive omen in a dream, as recorded in the *Bei Tang Shu Chao.*

Lightning and Thunder

**A portent of of good luck and blessings,
including the birth of a child.**

In the *Prince of Huai Nan* it states, "Thunder comes when Yin and Yang are interacting with each other." The *Book of the Later Han* says, "Thunder is a command from heaven and the earth; the virtues are thus born. Thunder enlightens the ignorant and defeats evil." Another text says, "Thunder belongs to the sky and earth and can mean the coming of a first child." It also says that thunder is the symbol of a human emperor and sages, as well as a symbol of ministers or princesses. So, interpreters generally considered thunder and lightning in dreams as good omens. A story in the *Book of the Northern Dynasty* relates that when Dou Tai's mother was pregnant she dreamed of the coming of a windy thunderstorm. She went out into the courtyard and saw lightning that looked like eyes and became drenched by the rain. When she awoke she found herself covered with perspiration. Much later her child Dou Tai became attained high rank and became rich.

The *Book of Songs* tells that when the mother of Zong Ze was giving birth, there was suddenly lightning and thunder and flashes of light covered her body. The next day she gave birth and her child became a great general

Zhang Si Yuan was loyally served by a tiger and its two cubs (Wang).

in the war against the Mongolians. He also appointed Yue Fei as his assistant general and together they won many victories; the people called him Zong Ye (Grandpa Zong) or Zong Fu (Father Zong) out of respect.

But dreams of lightning could also be interpreted as something bad, depending upon the dreamer. The *Meng Zhan Yi Zhi* says that after emperor Zhou of the Shang dynasty dreamed of thunder and lightning, he was struck by lightning and thus punished for his misdeeds.

Lion and Tiger

A dream of a lion or tiger portends gaining great power.

The tiger is regarded as the king of mountain beasts while the lion has a magnificent mane and shows unusual strength. Dreams of lions and tigers were seen as positive omens, symbols of nobility and power. Tigers are associated with the color white and the direction west.

The *Book of the Southern Dynasties* tells a story of Jing Ze, king of Qi, who dreamed he was riding a five-colored lion. Some time later, a new emperor came into power and Jing Ze was promoted to a high-ranking position. Another story in the *Gui Hua* tells that in the Ming dynasty one Chen You Ding was born into an impoverished family and worked as a servant in the Luo family. One day Chen lost a goose belonging to the master of the family. In fear of punishment, he ran to the Wang family, who provided him with emotional support. Master Wang had just had a dream in which he saw a tiger sitting at his door. He awoke just as Chen arrived and so believed that his dream was an omen. He felt that he had found the "tiger at his door" and arranged the marriage of his daughter to Chen, who later become very rich.

The *Shan Xi Tong Zhi* tells of a person named Liu Qian who lived in Gaoling during the Ming dynasty. Liu Qian was born into a very poor family and had no employment. However, he was asked to work one night as a stand-in for his sick brother, who was employed as a gong ringer, announcing the time of day to the inhabitants of the city. On that very night he substituted for his brother, the county governor had a dream in which he saw a white lion sitting under the gong. Awakened the next day, he went to the gong and saw Liu Qian. Reflecting upon what his dream portended, he sent Liu Qian to school. Liu Qian later became a provincial governor.

The New Collection of Zhou Gong's Dream Interpretations says "If one dreams of seeing tigers, it means that he will be promoted. If one dreams of seeing lions, it means that he will be noble and rich. However, lions and tigers are also symbols of violence since they kill and eat humans." Thus there is an evil aspect of lion and tiger dreams. In Chen Shi Yuan's book it says that because the tiger shows his violence by killing, especially in the fall, it is the most feared mountain beast and a sign of violence and misfortune.

Medicine

Bitter Medicine
A reminder that bitter medicine is generally good for one's health and soul.

The *Yong Zhuang Xia Pin* by Zhu Guo Zhi tells that the first emperor of the Ming dynasty, Zhu Yuan Zhan, had a dream in which he was given some medicine. He tasted it and found it particularly bitter, but he heard a voice that said that if he ate the medicine his spirit would be strengthened, his body would be healthier, and he would have a longer life. The interpreter further added that he would soon employ a loyal and able minister. And true enough, he soon appointed Zhou Shi Xiu as minister, who loyally assisted him in running the empire. Bitter medicine is thus good for the health and uncomfortable words may be good for the heart.

Special Medicine Pill
An omen of regaining one's sight.

The *Xu Yi Jian Zhi* records that a monk who had been blind for many years had a dream in which someone gave him a prescription. The directions for preparing the prescription were long and complicated, but when the monk awoke, he followed the detailed instructions as he remembered in his dream and regained his sight.

Mirror

An omen of having insight.

A mirror is said to reflect one's wisdom, heart, and internal qualities. A dream of a mirror is thus an indication of one's mental clarity and insight. As insight is considered as a positive attribute, interpreters considered the mirror as a positive omen. *The Book of the Southern Dynasty* tells the story of Dao Ji, whose son was named Jing (mirror) and took the literary name Yuanzhao (round-reflecting). This was because when Jing's mother was pregnant, she dreamed of carrying a round mirror *(jing)* in her chest. The boy grew to be both handsome and clever.

Another story tells that a man named Wang Chu Na dreamed he saw a man holding a large mirror with constellations on it. The man then cut open Wang's stomach and put the mirror inside him. He awoke and was puzzled by the dream, which he remembered for many years. Later in his life he became an expert on climate and astronomy, skills that dream interpreters believe were foretold by his dream.

A mirror is also thought to reflect or reveal secrets. In temples and palace buildings are usually huge boards with sayings regarding mirrors, such as *Qing tian ming jing,* meaning "Clear skies, bright mirrors." Another inscription, *Ming jing gao xuan,* or "Bright mirror hangs above," means that the master of the domain is without bias.

But the mirror is above all seen as a woman's possession. Interpreters often claimed that if a woman dreamed of a mirror and looked into it, the husband or relative who is far away would return. The typically round shape of a mirror symbolizes unity and gathering, while a broken mirror is a negative omen, indicating separation. This meaning has carried over into contemporary times and is held by the common people. *Po jing chong yuan,* "The broken mirror is round again" is a common expression meaning that there is peace after a crisis between husband and wife.

Looking into a Mirror

An omen of coming death.

In the *Jiu Tang Shu* is a story of Cui Tui, who was to be expelled from the country for a minor infraction. Before his expulsion, he had a dream that he looked into a mirror, but he didn't know what to make of this dream when he awakened. However, later, rather than being expelled, he was commanded by the emperor to be put to death despite his young age and the petty nature of his crime. The dream of looking into a mirror was thus seen as an omen of death.

Money

A dream of money is an omen of trouble.

Just as in the West money is said to be the "root of all evil," Chinese traditionally assumed that those who hoarded money would lose their righteousness and humanity. In the Jin dynasty it was the custom to never mention the word for money, *qian,* thereby avoiding damage to one's good character and generous nature. Dreaming of gathering great treasure would thus mean that the dreamer would soon quarrel with others and be hated. This was likely based on the realistic observation that those preoccupied with business and money were prone both to dream of money and to quarrel about financial matters, thereby causing themselves misery and worry. On the other hand, giving money away to others was seen as benevolent and this type of dream was a dream of good fortune.

The New Collection of Zhou Gong's Dream Interpretations records that "If one dreams of seeing gold or silver, he will have a debate or lawsuit. If one dreams of making money, he will have quarrels. But if one dreams of giving money away, he will receive a great fortune. If one dreams of seeing mutilated money, his quarrel will come to an end. If one dreams of finding money on the road, he will lose his fortune. If one dreams of having a huge amount of money or suddenly becoming rich, great evil and misfortune are coming."

Another text tells of Wang Dao, who dreamed that a man came to buy his oldest son, Wang Yue, for a million dollars. After this dream Wang Dao secretly prayed for the strength not to give in to such an offer. Not long afterward, he found a treasure worth a million dollars. Thinking that this was an evil omen, he hid the money and told no one. However, soon after, his eldest son became sick and died. The *Records of the Dark and the Bright* records a similar story.

Moon

A symbol of ministers and a portent of good fortune related to power.

The moon is related to various Yin elements, and symbolizes concubines, empresses, ministers, and subjects, the "opposites" of the Yang-related sun, heaven, and the emperor. In the *The Prince of Huai Nan,* the sun and moon are said to be the messengers of the heavens. In *The Book of Han,* it says that the moon is the most important of the various Yin elements, and may mean that "The female will become a concubine, empress, or a official."

Many dream interpreters believed that the moon could also mean extreme good fortune, especially for a woman. According to *The Book of Han,* Wang Mang's grandfather's wife once dreamed the moon came into her chest. She later gave birth to a daughter and the daughter became an empress. In *The Book of Songs,* Sun Jian's wife also dreamed while pregnant that the moon came into her chest and later give birth to the emperor Sun Ce. *The Biographies of the Early Sages in Hui Ji* tells that when Gan Ze was young, he dreamed that his name was shining on the moon. He later became a county official in charge of education. He was so knowledgeable and good that he was likened to the moon, pure and shining. According to *The Copied Books in Bei Tang Studio,* those who see the moon in their dreams become high-ranking officials.

The following well-known example is recorded in *Zuo Zhuan:* "When the two countries Jin and Chu were fighting each other, Lu Qi of Jin dreamed he shot at the moon with an arrow and hit it. Afterward he withdrew into the mud. The next day during the fighting he couldn't put this dream out of his mind. He sought out an interpreter, who told him that since Jin belonged to the descendants of the Zhou emperor, they were symbols of the sun, while the Chu were related to the moon. Shooting the moon in his dream meant that he would win the battle, while withdrawing into the mud meant that he himself would die and return to the earth. When the fighting again commenced, Lu Qi indeed shot the king of Chu in the eye with an arrow and killed him, while Lu Qi himself was shot by a minister of Chu and died.

Mother

Mother Becoming Ill
An omen of impending death.

Dreaming of one's mother becoming ill is a prediction of death. This is based on a story in the *Book of Yuan* which tells of Yi Xin, who went to the capital to study and one evening dreamed that his mother became ill. He felt uneasy and frightened when he awoke and went directly home to find his mother had already died.

Seeing Mother's Lower Body
An omen of findings one's path in life.

The *Tai Ping Guang Ji* tells a Tang dynasty story regarding a dream that included a vision of a mother's lower body. Tang Gu Zong was an official who had violated the law and was put into prison by order of the emperor, awaiting punishment that would certainly be a public beheading. Alone and filled with anxiety while awaiting his execution, he finally fell asleep and dreamed he saw his mother's lower body. Startled, he awoke and was even more fearful. By chance a dream interpreter saw him in his great despair, but to Tang Gu Zong's surprise the interpreter said that this was a dream of good luck and meant that he would not receive capital punishment. The interpreter said that to dream of the lower body of one's mother was to realize the path of one's life. At the moment of his death he would see once again the path of life. His dream was indeed a symbol of good fortune for the next day an important minister intervened for Tang Gu Zong and begged the emperor to spare his life. The emperor relented and Tang Gu Zong was released, later to become prime minister.

Mountain

A symbol of leaders and rulers.

Mountains were believed to symbolize emperors, kings, or sages. Before a ruler or sage died, it was not uncommon for some to have dreams of a mountain collapsing. On the other hand, dreams of mountains rising were

Ping Ao, the rain master, traveling with deer and Ao, a great sea turtle bearing magical island on its back (Xiao).

indications of being healed or becoming respected by others. *The Book of Rites* says, "Mountains can be worshiped as benevolent men *(ren)*." Chen Shi Yuan says that "Wang Chong's *On the Eternal* states that 'Mountains and hills and high platforms are the signs of high official position. Dreams of climbing up to those places will soon bring such high positions to the dreamers.' This should be believed."

The Book of Songs tells that Liu Mu Zhi once dreamed of taking a boat out to sea with emperor Wu Di. They encountered a huge storm but two dragons swam under the boat pulled it to a mountain, one so beautiful that the emperor was pleased. After the dream, Liu Mu Zhi was summoned by the emperor and was appointed to a position equivalent to internal prime minister. Another text states that if one dreams of wearing a mountain on his hat, it means that he will gain a fortune; while if one dreams that he is walking in a mountain forest, it also means a great fortune will come. Another source states that if one dreams of climbing mountains, he will receive a high appointment; if one dreams that he is going up to the mountain, everything that he desires will be attained but if the mountain collapses, it is an indication of impending evil.

A well-known example in *The Book of Jin* records that Zhang Zhai dreamed that he was riding a horse up to a mountain. Upon his return, he walked around his house three times and saw only pine trees; he couldn't find the door of the house to enter. He was told by a dream interpreter that his inability to find the door meant that he had no home and his walking three times around the house meant the disaster would come three years later. These omens proved to be true.

Music, Musical Instruments (see Singing)

Name Changing

An omen of fortune and position.

Changing one's name was seen as an important act that was done only in accordance with the will of gods or spirits. Scholars and sages believed that their names as well as their fortunes were matters of destiny; the names of those who passed the civil service examinations and obtained high rank were already in a book written by the gods. Interpreters believed that if one dreamed that his name was changed, it was done with god's wishes and the change corresponded to a change in heavenly fortune. It was also an indication that they would succeed in the civil service examination and be promoted to a higher rank.

Random Notes of the Qing Xiang Studio records: "A person named Sun Bian was previously named Sun Gu. Before taking his civil service examination, he dreamed of being in the residence hall of a high official late at night. Alone in the silent, empty hall, he found a book with a list of names lying on the table. It appeared that the list of names were of those who had achieved success in passing the examination. He went through the list without finding his own name but there was a blank space in the third highest position. He wanted to write his name in this blank space but suddenly he heard a voice told him that the name Sun Gui would not be on the list but the name Sun Bian would. Without thinking he wrote the name Sun Bian in the blank space. After he awoke he felt that this was an omen of good luck and so changed his name to Sun Bian. Sometime later he took the examination and to his surprise, he placed third and was later appointed to a high ministerial position.

The Records of the Predestined Fortune tells of a person named Doulu Shu, whose original name was Doulu Pu Zhen. When Doulu applied to take the upper level civil service examination, the local governor instructed him not to use two characters for his surname name but rather one, which is more common in Chinese. That night he had a dream in which an old man said that he should change his name to Shu, written with a character that has the meaning of "the fourth." After he awoke he accordingly changed his name to Doulu Shu. In his examination he placed fourth and was later appointed to the position of provincial governor.

Offering

Making an offering is a symbol of honoring the dead, which will bring rewards.

Making an offering is seen as a honorable act, and dreaming of making an offering is an omen of receiving a gift in gratitude for such an act. *The Book of Tea* by Lu Yu tells of a widow with two sons who lived in a house with a

Offerings being made to a cloud immortal riding a chariot pulled by a dragon (Xiao).

large enclosed garden. Inside the garden was an old tomb. Every time the widow prepared tea for herself and her sons, she would offer some to the tomb. The two sons complained that offering tea to the old tomb was foolish and wasteful, but the mother insisted. One night she dreamed a man said, "I have been in this tomb for over two hundred years and now your sons are going to damage it. It is because of you that I am protected and I will reward you." By morning, there were ten thousand pieces of money on the tomb and while the money looked old, the strings upon which it was strung were new. The mother told the sons of her dream and showed them the money. From that time forward they all lived a contented life.

Orchids

**The orchid represents elegance and nobility
and is believed to drive away evil.**

The orchid, *lan*, represents elegant beauty and high status, associations that have been carried down through the ages. For example even today people call their best friend *lan you* (orchid friend); an elegant room is a *lan shi* (orchid room); a lucky moment, *lan shi* (orchid moment); and so on. Moreover, the orchid is associated with jade and both are considered auspicious omens in dreams. If a pregnant woman dreamed of orchids, it meant that she would give birth to a noble son.

The Book of Zuo tells of an unfavored concubine of emperor Wen Gong of Zheng named Yan Ji, who dreamed her dead ancestors gave her orchids. They instructed her to use the fragrance of the orchids to obtain the love and admiration of the people of the country. After she had this dream, Yan Ji suddenly became favored by the emperor, who presented her with an orchid. Yan Ji and the emperor agreed that if they had a son, the orchid would be his symbol and, as fate would have it, she soon gave birth to a son and named him Prince Lan. Although the emperor had numerous offspring by numerous wives and concubines, Prince Lan was chosen to be the heir apparent and, in time, became the next emperor, Mu Gong.

Organs

Receiving a New Heart
Receiving a new heart is an omen of longevity.

The *Shi Yi Ji* records that emperor Shao Wang of the Zhou dynasty dreamed of a man clothed in feathers who came to him on a cloud to give him a new heart. The man said, "Your majesty, your wisdom and talents have not yet been used and you need a long life, which is difficult to obtain." The emperor kneeled and begged the man to teach him how to obtain it. The feathered man pointed at the emperor's heart and as the finger touched the chest of the emperor his heart exploded and the emperor awoke. He saw blood on his bed and felt sick. Days later, the dream returned, and the feathered man said, "I was going to change your heart when you collapsed" but now he gave the emperor a special medicine and said, "If you eat this, you will live long." Emperor Shao Wang reigned for a lengthy period and attributed his longevity to this dream.

Cutting Out the Heart
An omen of knowledge and literary talent.

The Song dynasty text *Yi Yuan* by Liu Ting Shu tells the story of Zheng Xuan, a well-known scholar of the Eastern Han dynasty. Zheng Xuan dreamed that he saw an old man cutting his heart out and placing ink in its place while stating, "Now you will have knowledge." The man disappeared. After the dream Zheng Xuan became more learned and full of miraculous insights to the admiration of many.

Intestines
Intestines in a dream indicate death.

Yang Xiong was a high official and famous general of the Han dynasty who dreamed of something coming out of his intestines. He asked several interpreters about his dream, but no one could enlighten him. The second day following the dream he died, and interpreters realized that this dream was an omen of his impending death.

Stomach and Heart
An omen of gaining wisdom.

Chinese believed the heart to be the central of the five organs and the center of the whole body. Thinking and wisdom were initiated from the heart. In *The Book of Internal Medicine* it is written, "The heart is the essence of the five organs." Also, in *The Book of Xun Zi,* it states, "The heart is the controller of the emperor and the source of heavenly wisdom." In *The Book of Guan Zi,* it also says "The heart is the organ where wisdom resides." To open one's heart in a dream came to mean that one was able to rid oneself of problems and to gain wisdom and insight. Interpreters believed that a dream of a knife cutting into the stomach or opening the heart were symbols of one's knowledge increasing.

A story in *Tai Ping Guang Ji* tells that, "Zheng Xuan studied for three years with his teacher, Ma Rong, but he was able to achieve little. The teacher was frustrated and thought Zheng Xuan was just stupid, so he sent him home. On the way back to his home, Zheng Xuan fell asleep under a tree and dreamed that an old man used a knife to cut open his heart. This elderly man told him that from then on he would learn scholarly things and achieve greatness in his life. Zheng Xuan awakened and returned to his teacher to tell him of this dream and begged to continue his studies. Ma Rong agreed and Zheng Xuan soon became an extremely knowledgeable person. He wrote many books and became a great master of classical literature. His teacher was so enthralled with Zheng Xuan's knowledge he later willed Zheng Xuan his prized collection of classical books."

The *New Tang History* records, "Since his youth Yi Zhi Zhang desired to learn but was unable to advance by simply reading books. He later dreamed he saw a man wielding a huge ax that cut open his heart, and into the cavity the man placed some herbs. The dream shocked him so that he awoke. However, after this dream he became more inquisitive and clever and became known for his great insight and wisdom."

The *Book of the Five Dynasties* records that a person from Luo Yang named Wang Chu Na dreamed that a man cut open his stomach and placed inside it a huge mirror inscribed with the constellations. He was so surprised that he awoke covered with perspiration. A month later he still felt pain in his stomach. However, from that day forward he became interested in the stars and in his later life became a great astronomer.

Cleansing and Changing the Inner Organs
An omen of increasing one's wisdom.

The early Chinese believed that wisdom, desire, and will all had their origin in the inner organs. *The Book of Internal Medicine* states that, "In the five organs there reside five spirits. In the liver is *hun,* a positive soul or ghost; in the heart there is *shen,* god or essence; in the lungs there is *yi,* desire and will; in the spleen, there is *po,* a negative soul or ghost; and in the kidney, there is *zhi,* ambition." This belief led to the idea that cleansing or changing the inner organs would improve one. A dream of organs being changed or cleansed meant that the spirits of those organs would be cleansed and increased wisdom would follow.

The *Ethnography of Hang Zhou* says that in the city of Qian Tang lived a one named Feng Jun, who at age eighteen dreamed that the Heavenly Emperor sent gods to change his lungs. When he awoke he felt cleverer, more inquisitive, and and full of knowledge. Without studying he later became an expert in classical literature and could predict the fortune of others. Even though he stayed within the walls of his house, it was said that his spirits traveled the seas and he could control waves and storms at will. He died at an old age without any illness.

Another story records that Wang Ren Yu dreamed that he was cut open and his stomach was washed with the water of the West River. He dreamed that all the sand, stone, and rocks became the shape of *zhuan shu,* a style of calligraphy. Wang's writing progressed to the point where he was promoted to the position of minister and in this position he became a friend of the son of the future emperor.

Spitting Out Five Organs
An omen of overuse of organs, resulting in death.

This type of dream refers to stress on the internal organs due to worrying, sadness, or extreme anxiety, which cause the organs to leave the body. *The New Views of Huan Tan* tells of Yang Xiong, who was called upon by the emperor Cheng Di of the Han dynasty to write a prose-poem *(fu)* entitled "Gan Quan Fu" (Ode to the Sweet Fountain). As Yang Xiong was working, he became tired, and soon fell asleep. He dreamed that his five organs left his body and were scattered on the floor. He picked them up and placed them with his own hands into his abdomen. After he awoke he felt tired and lacked energy. He became sick and less than a year later died.

The *Meng Zhan Yi Zhi* records the story of a Northern Qi dynasty scholar-official named Li Guang, who dreamed he saw a person come out of his body and say to him, "You have overused your heart so much that now I have to say goodbye to you." The person then left, and soon afterward Li Guang became sick and died.

Thus dreams about the five organs leaving the body are interpreted as indicating overuse and thereby abuse of the body. Scholars energetically studied the classics, philosophy, and arts, in an effort to achieve perfection, and their behavior sometimes became radical. They even tied their hair to the ceiling beams or stabbed their buttocks with needles to remain alert while studying, behavior expressed in idioms of today referring to great effort: *tou xuan liang* (tying the hair to the roof beam) and *zhui ci gu* (stabbing the buttocks with a needle). Seeing the five organs leave the body is an expression of the hard work required for great learning. *The Literary Heart and the Carving of Dragons* states, "Even when one spits out his heart and his bladder, it is not enough to say that this is the end."

Palace

Portends a great change in one's future.

As the location of the imperial court or the residence of the imperial family, the palace is a symbol of the emperor and the state. Interpreters considered dreams of palaces to be favorable, indicating a future promotion. *The Book of the Southern Dynasty* relates that long before the first emperor of Qi was chosen to be emperor, he dreamed that he saw himself climbing the steps of the imperial palace while wearing evening slippers made of mulberry wood. This dream was interpreted for him by Geng Wen, who pointed out that the character for this particular type of wood, *sang,* is the character for forty with two extra dots. This meant that at the age of forty-two, he would become the emperor. And such was the case.

But palaces can have other interpretations. It is said that if one dreams of traveling to a ghostly or heavenly palace, it means that they are called by the ghost and will die soon. One text relates the story of Fang Chao, who had just recovered from an illness but then had a relapse. In his delirium he dreamed he saw a palace, and a Daoist monk called to him, saying "You originally were supposed to be a great servant of the Heavenly Emperor, but by mistake you were sent to the earth. You will soon return to the heavens." Fang died soon afterward. *The Notes from Dong Xuan* tell of Wang Ping Pu, who once dreamed that he was traveling to the Ling Zhi (a sacred fungus) Palace when he heard a voice that said that soon he would be there. After he awoke, he felt uncomfortable and could not get this dream out of his mind. He never truly recovered and four years later he died.

Pavilion

An omen of success in one's achievements.

The use of walls for protection has deep roots in Chinese history. Pavilions were usually located on the walls of a city or within them. The *Tai Ping Yu Lan,* states, "The city or its walls and pavilions refers to the human ruler. Dreams of seeing a city means the dreamer will soon see the ruler, emperor, or king. If one sees a newly built city in a dream, he will become famous and his achievements will be great." The pavilion is also identified as a symbol of accumulated achievement. "If one dreams of a pavilion, it means that he is building his virtue and achievement. In contrast, if one dreams that the pavilion is damaged or destroyed, it means that one's luck has run out."

As city walls and the pavilions on them were high, views from the walls were spectacular. As a result, both pavilions and walls in dreams represent both power and magnificence. Going up these old walls and pavilions were dreams of good fortune, indicating that one would be given an official title. "Seeing pavilions and palaces in dreams is a good omen. Dreams of going upstairs in a pavilion will bring a title of higher rank to the dreamers."

Peach

A safeguard against evil and an omen of longevity.

The appearance of the peach in a dream is a favorable omen. The fruit was a favorite of Xi Wang Mu, the Queen Mother of the West, who invited chosen favorites to partake of her special peaches to acquire immortality. This Daoist tale carries over to interpretations regarding the peach in dreams. However, peaches in dreams can also mean protection from evil influences and the maintenance of official positions, the latter recorded in the *Tai Ping Yu Lan*.

Peacock

An omen of brilliant literary skills.

The Book of the Southern Dynasties tells that when emperor Qi Wu was young, he had a dream in which he saw someone take up a brush pen and draw two wings on his body and fine clothes made of peacock feathers, enabling him to fly up into the sky. Qi Wu did not know what to make of this strange dream but one of his ministers, Geng Wen, said that the bird was a symbol of official rank and the colorful clothes were an indication of literary ability, thus confirming the emperor's opinion of his nobility and talent.

The peacock is a beautiful bird said to have five colors, and has traditionally been considered a sign of literary brilliance. *The Book of Songs* tells of Bo Si, a bright young man who dreamed that a peacock landed in his family's garden. After waking up he felt compelled to write a poem, which was praised for its elegant words. Bo Si later passed the highest level of civil examination and became a minister of education.

Pearl

Together with jewelry and jade, pearls are treasures of the rich and noble and thus signs of wealth and status.

Both pearls and jade are symbols of purity and virtue. Pearls appearing in a dream are omens of nobility or exalted position, the reward of virtue. *The Book of Songs* tells of a woman who dreamed that a man presented her pearls of five different colors before giving birth to a son named Yue Shi. The boy studied diligently and passed his examinations. In the Southern Tang period, he received the position of first place in the national examination, and in the Song period, he also passed the national examination with a high mark and became a high-ranking official.

A story is also recorded about the mother of Xi Shi (regarded as one of the most beautiful women in Chinese history), who once dreamed that she was covered with a light reflected from pearls and jade. She later became pregnant and gave birth to Xi Shi, who grew up to be the renowned beauty.

Stories Passed Down from the Kai Yuan Era tells that Zhang Sui's mother once dreamed of a jade swallow flying into her chest. She became pregnant and later gave birth to a boy, Zhang Sui, who became the prime minister.

Pen (Brush Pen)

An omen of great intellectual ability and literary skills.

Dreams involving pens or brushes for writing are frequently associated with sages or nobles. *The New Tang History* tells of Li Jiao, a son of great filial piety, who served his mother faithfully. One evening, he dreamed that a sage gave him two brush pens. In later life he became famous for his ability to write wonderful essays and poems.

A Song dynasty story concerns the mother of of Fan Zhi, who, before giving birth to her son dreamed that she saw a sage give her a five-colored brush pen. When Fan Zhi was nine years old, he could already compose poetry and when he was thirteen his reading skills were those of an adult scholar. He passed the highest level of the civil service examination, called *jin shi,* and had many students who sought his instruction. Finally he was appointed prime minister and was given the title Prince of Lu.

Another story in *The Book of the Southern Dynasty* tells that Ji Shao Yu had a dream in which Lu Chui gave him a black-handled pen. Lu Chui said that the pen was a good one and told Ji Shao Yu to do good things. After this dream Ji Shao Yu's writings improved greatly as did his imagination.

In contrast to the good omen of receiving a brush, if a person is asked to return a brush in a dream, it is considered a bad omen, meaning that person's imagination or literary creative ability was diminishing. A variation of this interpretation explains that *bi,* for "brush pen," has the same pronunciation as *bi* meaning "end." Sometimes the brush pen dream is thus interpreted to mean the end of life. In the *Notes from the Studio Lao Xue An,* Zhong Gong Gong dreamed he was given a brush pen by the emperor Hui Zong of the Song dynasty. He wrote a poem and essay to remember the occasion but afterward became sick and never rose again.

Another example in *The Book of Jin* tells that Wang Xun once dreamed that he was given a large brush pen, as big as a roof beam. He awoke and told others "This must mean that my writing ability should improve greatly." Soon after the emperor died and there were many edicts to be written, most all of which were written by Wang Xun.

A brush pen blossoming is an unusual variation. *The Strange Stories in the Years of Kai Yuan Tian Bao* tells that, "When Li Taibai [Li Bai, regarded as China's greatest classical poet] was young, he had a dream in which the brush pen he was using suddenly blossomed. Later his reputation was indeed spread throughout the universe." This story is also recorded in the *Speech Garden.*

Phoenix

The phoenix is synonymous with success.

The phoenix is a mythical five-colored bird of great auspiciousness, the most supreme of all flying animals, and possessing both virtue and benevolence. According to Yi Wen "If the five elements are in perfect harmony and each makes its beautiful sound, then the phoenix will come. Both the male and female phoenix have the crown of a chicken, the beak of a swallow, a neck like a snake, the wings of a Qilin, scales of a dragon, tail of a fish, and five colors. It does not eat live animals." According to *The Book of Mountains and Seas,* the phoenix looks like a crane and has five-colored feathers on its body. "The female phoenix is called *feng;* its head represents virtue, its wings represent success, its back represents righteousness, its neck represents benevolence, and its chest represents loyalty. This bird sings and dances by itself. If one sees the phoenix, it means the whole universe is at peace."

A story in *The Book of Songs* says that when Duan Shao Lian's mother was pregnant she dreamed of a female phoenix in the yard. After the dream she gave birth to a boy, who grew up to be a handsome, elegant young man with great knowledge and abilities. He later became an official in charge of education. Another story in the book *Wu Dai* records that "When Xu Ling's mother was pregnant she dreamed that she saw something of five colors turn into a phoenix, which then landed on her shoulder. She later gave birth to Xu Ling." A monk who touched the boy's head said that the boy was a Qilin that came down from the sky. When Xu Ling grew up his knowledge was incomparable.

Xiao Qi, who was able to attract phoenixes by playing his flute (Wang).

Because the phoenix has five-colored feathers that are very bright, interpreters consider a phoenix dream to be an omen of a literary personage capable of writing superb essays and poems. A story in the *Book of Jin* tells that when Luo Han was young became orphaned and was raised by his uncle and aunt. He had a dream in which he saw a bird with colorful feathers that suddenly flew into his mouth. He was so surprised and startled by this dream that he woke up and told the story to his aunt, who said that the bird had literary colors and was an omen that later he would write brilliantly. His future did bring him fame as a poet and as a writer.

Phoenixes Alighting on Two Fists
An omen of impending death.

A Collection of Strange Stories tells of a person named Sun, who desired to become an official. He had a dream in which two phoenixes flew to him and alighted on his two fists. When he awoke he was baffled by this dream and went to an interpreter, who said, "Usually, the phoenix rests on the *wutong* (Chinese parasol) tree. So for you to dream that two phoenixes alighted on your two fists, I am afraid portends bad luck. Either you will grow and use a cane or you will cut a cane or stick to hold in each hand. This portends the death of your parents."

Holding a cane in as a portent of death has its origins in an ancient Confucian custom whereby a son holds a stick or cane in his hands for a specified period following the death of his parents. Upon the death of one's father, one held a stick of bamboo while upon the death of the mother, one held a stick made from the Chinese parasol tree. Thus the dream foretold that Sun would lose both parents, an omen which turned out to be true.

Phoenix Speaking
The phoenix speaks to predict the future.

The Random Notes on the Western Capital, by Ge Hong of the Jin dynasty, records that a scholar student named Yang Xiong had a dream in which he was reading and heard the voice of someone behind him. When he turned, he found that the voice came from not a person but from a white phoenix. The phoenix said that Yang Xiong would write a book called *Tai Xuan Jing*

(Book of Extremes), and then disappeared. Yang Xiong never forgot this strange dream. Much later in his life he became a learned scholar and did indeed write a book of that title, as predicted.

Pig

A dream of a pig has the meaning of being honored.

According to the *Tai Ping Yu Lan,* a large pig known to the people of Yan as the "god of the pigs" and said to be 120 years old was dedicated to the king of Yan. Because the emperor was told by his prime minister that the pig was old and useless, the emperor told the people to slaughter the pig and eat it. When the pig was killed, it appeared in the dream of the prime minister and said, "Now that you have helped me to be transformed from a worldly life into a spirit, I can now serve people with my body as precious food. In honor of your benevolence, I will reward you." Later when the prime minister traveled to Lu, he was given a precious pearl held in the mouth of a red turtle, an extremely high honor.

Hunting Pig
Hunting pig is an omen of success and victory.

The *Bei Qi Shu* records a story of Zhao Yan Shen of northern Qi, who was fighting for the emperor of Wei. As the battle was in progress and there was serious danger of losing, the prime minister told Zhao "Yesterday I had a dream that we were hunting a herd of pigs and I killed all of them except the largest one. I couldn't do it and you said 'You can do it' and indeed I suceeded with this hunting knife. Can such a dream come true?" He then presented Zhao his knife and said, "Now I will give you this to ensure our victory." Zhao thankfully took the knife and went into battle. Single-handedly his ferocious fighting turned the tide and led to victory.

Pine

A pine tree can have both positive and negative meanings.

Pine trees are one of the most common designs depicted in Chinese art. As they remain green throughout the winter, they are a symbol of strength and endurance. As such, they are depicted frequently alone or as one of the so-called three friends of winter, i.e., pine, plum, and bamboo. When pine trees appear in dreams, they may symbolize strength. However, they also have negative connotations, since they grow in graveyards. Dreams of pine trees can thus be omens of impending death.

A story from the Three Kingdoms period tells that Ding Gu, prime minister of the Wu, once dreamed he saw a pine tree growing out of his stomach. He later told his dream to others saying, "The character for pine tree, *song*, is the combination of the words 'eighteen' and 'kings.' It means that I will be king in eighteen years." This dream was later proved true and is an example of interpreting dreams based on the analysis of characters.

A dream of a pine tree growing in front of one's house is an ill omen, meaning that death will arrive. *The Notes from You Yang* tells of an official named Yang Song Ji, who was known to be good at interpreting dreams. When someone came to him to seek his advice, saying that he had dreamed he saw pine trees growing in front of the door, another person who was listening said that he had dreamed of date trees growing on his house. Yang interpreted both dreams, saying, "Pine trees grow in the cemetery, so if they grow in front of the house, it means that death will come. The date tree, *zao*, growing upon the house has a similar meaning. The character for the date tree has the meaning of repeating. This refers to a calling from the roof, a ritual for the dead person's soul to be called from the house to go up to the roof." Soon after the interpretation, those two people both died.

Plant

See Bamboo, Pine, Plum

Plum

An omen of worry.

Dreams involving a plum tree are a sign of coming worries and concerns. The *Tai Ping Yu Lan* states that the plum is a sign of worrying about being assigned duties as a prison officer.

Pomegranate (see Fruit)

Pregnancy

Pregnancy by Relations with a Spirit
A dream of nobility or high position.

In this dream a woman has sexual relations with a spirit or a god, and becomes pregnant. These dreams were believed to portend great fortune or coming preferment for high office or title as they demonstrated direct communication between the subject and either a spirit or god. *The Book of Han* states that when the mother of the first emperor of the Han dynasty was resting on a hill, she drifted off to sleep and dreamed she had sexual relations with spirits. She was awakened by lightning and thunder and and the skies became dark. When her husband came upon her, he saw a dragon holding her. Soon she learned that she was pregnant and later gave birth to Liu Bang, the first emperor of the Han dynasty. Liu Bang claimed that a dragon fathered him and this story is sometimes claimed as being the origin of the dragon as the symbol of the emperor.

It is said that the mother of Confucius, Zheng Zai, once dreamed that the Black Heavenly Emperor sent a messenger requesting her to come to him. In her dream she had relations with the black emperor and was told that she would give birth to a child in an empty forest. After she woke up, she had a premonition that she was pregnant and later gave birth to Confucius.

The Grand History tells that early during the early reign of the Yellow Emperor, a huge star fell like a rainbow on the Hua Zhu area (the central plain of China). A young virgin living where the star fell dreamed she that she had relations with the rainbow, and immediately sensed that she was pregnant. She later gave birth to emperor Shao Hao.

Punishment (see Beheading)

Qilin (Kylin or Kirin)

A symbol of good luck.

The imaginary beast called Qilin is a sign of peace and prosperity, and dreams of Qilin were considered auspicious. The *Book of Jiang Nan* tells that during the Ming dynasty in Tu County lived a person known as Shao Meng Lin. When his mother was pregnant she had a dream that she gave birth to a Qilin. When she awoke, she was not disturbed by this strange dream but did not understand its meaning. She gave birth to a boy and named him Meng Lin, meaning "Dream of a Qilin." Meng Lin attained the highest level of *jin shi* in the national civil service examination and became the vice-governor of the county of Shen Jen. Another book, the *Xiao Jing*, records that Confucius had a dream in which he saw a little boy beating a Qilin with a willow branch. The boy injured the precious animal's left foot, so Confucius, in an effort to treat the injury, covered the foot with grass and wood chips. The Qilin spit out three books to Confucius, who studied them with great diligence.

Quail

Expresses the wishes or desires of the common people.

A Song dynasty text tells that Cai Jing, a prime minister who liked to eat quail, dreamed one night that a quail came to accuse him of abusing his authority. Waking up and reflecting, he thought the dream frivolous and meaningless. Later, however, he was overthrown in a popular rebellion because he lived such a luxurious life while the common people suffered. The quail has since been interpreted as representing the common people.

A princess of the court of the Queen Mother of the West, riding a Qilin (Wang).

Quince (see Fruit)

Rain

A portent of being bestowed with blessings and riches.

Rain was believed to be a blessing from the heavens, as it provided the nourishment necessary for the growth of crops. *A General Record of the Emperor He Tu* states that "Rain is a blessing from the heaven." Interpreters therefore considered dreams in which there was rain or where one was rained upon as a fortunate omen of a patronage by the emperor, along with which would come official position and riches. The *Records of Baoguang* tells of two gentlemen named Wang and Xu, who both sought the position as governor of the county. Wang dreamed that he was walking in the rain with his hat on, while Xu dreamed that he was traveling on a river and was struck by lightning. The two asked for the dreams to be interpreted by the well-known dream interpreter Ye Guang Yuan, who predicted that Wang would not become an official because he wore his hat in the rain, thereby preventing the rain from striking him; that is, he was not blessed by the emperor. Xu's dream on the other hand was interpreted positively, as he was struck by the lightning, meaning he would get the official position. This interpretation turned out to be true for both.

Rain is also felt to facilitate Yin Qi being connected above and Yang Qi being connected below. Rain is related to the category of Yin phenomenon and occurs when the Qi cannot be connected. If one has a Yin rain dream, it meant that his Yin Qi is excessive and his body will become diseased. *The Remaining Books of Dunhuang* state that "If one dreams that it rains on a gloomy day, he will become sick."

The same text further states that, "If one dreams that it is raining in the spring or summer, it is a fortunate omen. If one dreams that it is raining in the autumn or winter it is an evil omen." This interpretation is based in the fact that spring and summer rain is good for growth and therefore beneficial. However in winter and fall, the rain is harmful to the stored harvest and brings dampness and chill to human habitation; it therefore is a symbol of difficulty or disaster.

Rainbow

An evil portent indicating conflict and confusion.

The rainbow was considered as an evil ghostly vapor on the side of the sun. It is said to be Yang inside of Yin and to indicate that the ministers, concubines, and empresses will have difficulty or will cause difficulty. The *Huai Nan Zi* states that "The rainbow is the Yang inside the Yin." *The Book of Jin,* on the other hand, states that the rainbow is an evil female vapor. One kind of rainbow is called *hong ni,* the vapor on the side of the sun, and it is believed that to oppose it will cause disruption of life energy. Therefore the rainbow was seen to be a symbol of confusion, internal conflict, usurpation, infidelity by one's spouse, or even the overthrow of the emperor.

Interpreters considered rainbow dreams to be symbols of unrest caused by disloyal ministers. The *Ethnography of Huayang* tells the story of Li Te's wife, Luo, who had a dream in which she saw two rainbows rising into the sky. One rainbow was broken in the middle. Her dream was interpreted to mean that one of her two sons would die early, and the other would become rich and noble. It did come to pass that her eldest son, Li Ying, died, while the second son, Li Xiong, established a kingdom in the southwest.

Rebirth (Returning to the Womb)

A portent of carrying the wishes of another.

Dreams of being reborn relate to folk tales of the rebirth of immortals or early famous nobles. *An Enlarged Collection of Strange Stories* tells of a lower ranking official named Yue Shi who dreamed that the Heavenly Emperor called to him. When he walked toward the sound of the emperor's voice, he found a beautiful palace. The voice said, "Your master wants to have a descendant and now you go to be reborn. Do not disappoint me and do not say no." He begged not to be sent but the Heavenly Emperor refused to relent and he was therefore compelled to follow orders. The servants standing by said that he was the bare-footed Immortal Li from the Southern

Mountain who got drunk and thus violated heavenly rules. As a result of his overindulgence he was ordered to go down to the lower world as punishment. A year later, the emperor on earth had a son who became Ren Zong, the emperor of the Song dynasty. This was the rebirth of Yue Shi, who was sent by the Heavenly Emperor.

A Collection of Song [dynasty] Poems says that when Xiang Zheng was born his mother dreamed that Li Bai, the famed poet of the Tang dynasty, was coming to visit her. At an unusually young age, Xiang Zheng gained fame in poetry. The well-known scholar-official Mei Yao Chen praised his poetry highly and told others that Xian Zheng was rebirth of Li Bai.

In *A Collection of the Things Seen and Heard,* it says that when Xu Peng Ju was born, his mother dreamed that she saw a general coming to their house. The general identified himself as Yue Fei (Yue Peng Ju), who led the war against the Mongolians in the Song dynasty, and stated that he had suffered for three generations and wanted to be reborn to have happiness and fortune. The mother named her newborn boy Peng Ju, after Yue Fei's literary name, and he later became the prince of Wei.

Road

Dreams of roads were considered omens of connection.

If the roads appearing in dreams are not blocked, everything will proceed smoothly. If one dreams of roads that are blocked, there will be difficulties in proceeding with one's plans. Chen Shi Yuan's book explains that if one was not to be successful in his efforts, he would dream of roads being impaired by swamps, mud, or other obstructions.

The Book of the Southern Dynasty relates that Kong Yu was thinking of invading the city of Jian Kang (today's Nanjing). However, he had a dream in which he was walking along the Xuan Yang Men (the imperial walkway). While looking ahead, he suddenly saw hills and mounds in the roadway obstructing his path and, unable to continue, he returned home. Disturbed by the dream, he realized that the rising mounds and hills were an ill omen telling him that the invasion of Jian Kang would be difficult.

Roof Tile (Falling)

An omen of bad luck.

The History of the Three Kingdoms relates that one day emperor Wen Di of Wei told his minister Zhou Xuan, "I saw in a dream two tiles falling from the palace roof. The two tiles became two birds, mandarin ducks. What does this mean?" Zhou Xuan answered, "It means that somebody in the back palace (where the empress and concubines live) died suddenly." Wen Di then said, "Actually, I didn't have this dream, but was only testing you." Zhou Xuan said, "A dream is the intention of the gods in heaven directing the living. If one's heart or mind are alive, then images conveyed from the gods portend good or bad luck whether through dreams or other thoughts." Before he finished speaking, a messenger entered to report to the emperor that a concubine had died as a result of a fight with another concubine.

Here we have not only an example of a tile falling from the roof, an omen of bad luck, but also mandarin ducks and roof tiles as females symbols. It was believed that roof tiles, which were made of clay, were a sign of the female and while jade items were symbols of the male. These symbols were also assumed to portend the gender of an unborn baby.

Rooster (see Chicken)

Scale

A symbol of riches and power.

Scales are used to measure weight as well as to assess the difference in weight between two objects. Interpreters considered the scale to symbolize riches and power as well as a judgment of relative merit.

The New Tang History records that when Shangguan Shao Rong was born, her whole family, except her grandfather and mother, were executed for violating the law. Her grandfather was a high-ranking official in the court; her mother, before giving birth to her, pretended to be a maid and thus survived. Before Shangguan was born, her mother dreamed she was given a large scale telling her to measure the universe. The mother thus thought her child would certainly be a boy, but to her great disappointment, a girl was born. When the child was fourteen, empress Wu Ze Tian of the Tang dynasty took her into her service, and she then drafted many edicts for the empress. When the next emperor, Zhong Zong, came into power, the girl was appointed a high official in charge of literature and music and was greatly favored.

On the other hand, dreams in which a scale is broken portend that one will lose power or even be killed. *A Collection of the Unusual* tells that "A person named Zong once dreamed that a huge scale of ten thousand *jin* was hanging on the roof. But soon the scale was broken in the middle. Zong felt uncomfortable about this dream and the same year he died." The *Tai Ping Yu Lan* explains, "A scale is used to measure one's treasure, one's sense of justice, or one's royalty, power, or fairness. The heavier the weight, the more noble the person. If power is lost or broken, the scale is broken as well."

Seal

A symbol of rank and status.

Since all officials who held rank used a seal to execute their orders, the seal was a symbol of power. Dream interpreters considered it an omen of official rank. One text tells that during the Later Han period of the Five Dynasties, Gao Fang resigned his position and stayed at home. He then dreamed an official came to visit him carrying a white bag. The bag contained a seal wrapped in a large piece of white cloth. The official gave the seal to Gao Fang and left without uttering a word. When Gao Feng awoke he was perplexed by the dream, realizing that the color white was a symbol of death. Not long after, the state of Zhou was established and, although he was retired, Gao Fang was called to serve as the minister of justice.

Another story tells of Ling Ce, who when he took office had a dream of someone carrying six seals and one sword, which were given to Ling Ce. Over his his lifetime, he came to serve six different official positions. A similar story tells that Liu Zi once dreamed of swallowing fourteen seals, and in real life, he held fourteen official positions.

Sex (see Intercourse)
Shaving

Shaving the beard portends excellence.

The *Qing Xiang Za Ji* tells that Li Di, who lived during the Song dynasty, dreamed his entire beard was shaved off. An interpreter told him that it was a positive omen, meaning that he would be first in whatever he endeavored to accomplish. He later won first place in the civil service examinations, the most coveted prize of all scholars.

Shoe (see Clothing and Accessories)
Singing (Dancing and Music)

A sign of sadness.

Although one would think dreams of singing and dancing would happen when one is happy and therefore would portend happiness, they are, in fact, usually interpreted as meaning just the opposite. *The Book of Lie Zi* states "Those who dream of drinking wine are in reality those who are sad; those who dream of singing and dancing are those who are crying." Chen Shi Yuan claims in his book, "When a person is about to cry, have a quarrel with others, or get involved in a lawsuit, he may have a dream of singing and dancing." In a similar vein, in *The New Collection of Zhou Gong's Dream Interpretations* it is written that "Those who dream of dancing are fearful. Those who have dreams of singing will quarrel with others."

These contrary interpretations may result from the influence of Confucian teachings, which hold that those who sing and dance to excess have lost control and therefore do not display true Confucian virtues. Interpreters were greatly influenced by Confucian ideals and therefore provided guidance in accordance with them. An educated person should exert self-control and not be preoccupied with singing and dancing.

On the other hand, playing music and musical instruments had good

Ji Kang, communicating with the spirits of music (Wang).

Zai Fu Ren, a female immortal in the guise of a weaving girl (Wang).

connotations, a view also in accord with traditional beliefs. *The Book of Filial Piety* says, "To change behavior, there is no better way than through music." The ancient Chinese considered music as a tool for educating people, and therefore dreams of musical instruments were considered good omens. *The Copied Books in Bei Tang Studio* states that, "Flutes are symbols of establishing relationships and thus dreams of flutes indicate one will soon have good friends." Thus interpreters claimed that musical instruments appearing in a dream portended good luck. As a matter of fact, playing musical instruments was always a virtue praised by Confucianism; Confucius himself was supposed to have edited a *Book of Music,* now lost. Playing a musical instrument, playing chess, composing poems and essays, practicing calligraphy, and painting were standard studies for becoming a scholar-official in ancient times.

Silk

Silk or embroidered cloth portends wealth, elegance, and nobility.

Silk was considered the finest cloth and was unaffordable by ordinary people, as was fine embroidered fabric. Therefore, dreams of silk and embroidered cloth are similar to dreams of fine food and are interpreted as signs of good fortune. Even today, people say *Yi jin huan xiang,* literally, "Returning home with silk clothes," as a expression for becoming rich.

Chen Shi Yuan wrote "When one is about to be blessed or favored by the Emperor, he will dream of silk clothes." Another text tells the story of Xue Xia, who lived in Tianshui during the Wei dynasty. When Xue Xia's mother was about to give birth, she dreamed someone presented her with a set of silk clothes, and told her that she would have a clever son who would be important to the emperor. When Xue Xia grew up, he was appointed minister of education. His brilliance was such that the emperor Wen Di liked to converse with him and even took off his fine silk robe and gave it to him. Thus his mother's dream came true.

For literary men, *jin,* embroidered silk cloth, meant elegance or eloquence in the use of words. Thus embroidered silk in a dream indicates great literary skills. *A Random Note on the Cloud Immortals* tells of Xiao Ying Shi of the Tang dynasty, who when he was young dreamed that someone presented him with embroidered flowers and pieces of silk. Following this dream his writing skills improved greatly and he won first place in the national level of the civil service examination. *The Book of the Southern Dynasty* tells of Jiang Yan, who was known for his literary talents even as a youth. He had a dream in which a man called Zhang Jing Yang came to him and said, "I once asked you to keep a bolt of silk for me, and now I would like you to please return it." Jiang Yan then fumbled and took out a piece of silk from under his clothes, but there were only a few feet of silk left of the whole bolt. Zhang became angry and accused Jiang Yin of using too much of it for himself. He then took the remaining silk and gave it to someone else. Jiang Yan's literary skills remained great but never improved over what they had been before.

See also Clothing and Accessories

Skeleton

**Dreaming of and conversing with a skeleton is a sign
of understanding true happiness and transcendence.**

The book of *Zhuang Zi* records that Zhuang Zi dreamed of seeing and conversing with a skeleton. There have been many interpretations of this incident. Daoists felt that the dream was related to a worldly life full of worries, and that true happiness only comes from going from the actual world into the nether world. Interpreters of many dynasties have explained this dream as a sign of understanding life and death, and understanding happiness in death.

Sky

A dream of the sky portends riches and power.

To the ancient Chinese, sky, or heaven, *(tian)* represented the ultimate Yang, and was variously known as the ancestor of ten thousand things *(wan wu zhi zu)*, the king of a hundred gods *(bai shen zhi jun)*, and the ruler of the mankind *(ren zhi zhu zai)*. Sky also controls speech and reason, and thus is the ruler of human beings. With such associations, it is only natural that the sky came to symbolize emperors and the highest virtues. Seeing the sky in a dream was considered an indication of respect and a sign of nobility. Ultimately it was a sign that the dreamer would become an emperor. Dreams of this kind were recorded in dynastic histories, perhaps reinforcing the belief that an emperor was chosen by the sky or heaven.

The empress Deng, wife of the emperor He of the Han dynasty once dreamed of climbing a ladder to the sky and knocking at the door of sky itself. In the dream the entire sky was wobbly but she saw something that appeared like huge stalactites, and looking up, she sucked on them. When she awoke she summoned the dream interpreter, who said, "Yao [one of the five sage emperors of a mythical past] once dreamed of climbing to the sky and then stopped; Tang [first emperor of the Shang dynasty] dreamed of reaching the sky and licking it. In both instances the dreamers came to rule the empire." *Records of the Han Dynasty* records that emperor Wu Di had dreamed of riding a red dragon up to the sky. He asked Feng Yi about this dream, who said, "This is a command from the sky through spirits." He later established his empire in Luoyang and the Han dynasty prospered.

Ministers and subjects also sometimes dreamed of the sky. Interpreters saw this dream as an indication of becoming physically close to the emperor, the "son of heaven" *(tian zi)*, thus an omen of becoming rich and gaining high position. *A Garden of the Unusual* relates that Liu Mu Zhi once dreamed of combining two boats to make one big ship, which he used to ascend to the sky. An old woman told him that "This means you will be sitting at the side of the emperor." Liu Mu Zhi later became a high-ranking general as his dream foretold. *The Book of Jin* records that Tao Kan of the Jin dynasty once dreamed of growing eight wings, which he used to fly up to the sky. As he was flying upward, he passed through eight of nine gates, but was unable to enter the last gate. He remembered this dream throughout his career, as he passed through eight levels of promotion to became a high-ranking official.

Not only was the sky a symbol of nobility of the highest order, it was also a place for the souls of the dead. Therefore, a dream of going to the sky might also be interpreted as an omen of death or becoming a hermit. *The Book of Zuo* tells the story of emperor Jing of the Jin dynasty, who became ill and died suddenly while using the toilet. Early that same morning, his servant had a dream in which he carried the emperor on his back and climbed into the sky. In reality, at noon of the same day, he carried the dead emperor out of the toilet on his back. The servant was subsequently buried with the emperor, a custom of the time that was regarded as a great honor.

There are still other interpretations regarding this dream symbol. *The Remaining Books of Dunhuang* states that "Dreams of seeing people coming from the sky is extremely auspicious; dreaming of going up to the sky is a good omen and the dreamer will have a precious son; dreaming of a hot sky means there will be war; dreaming of cloudy and rainy day indicates the dreamer will become ill." *The New Collection of Zhou Gong's Dream Interpretations* says, "One who has a dream of going up to the sky will have a precious son; a dream of bright sky will bring the dreamer good luck; seeing someone looking at the sky will give the dreamer longevity; seeing the sky will bring a fortune to the dreamer; and lastly, seeing the sky falling indicates that there will be famine."

Snake

Many meanings are possible but most feel that it portends evil.

The snake has a shape similar to a dragon. The *Hong Fan* says that the snake belongs to the dragon family and that a dragon without horns is a snake. Therefore, snake dreams were by many as portents of becoming noble. The snake, however, belongs to Yin, while dragons belong to Yang, so in that sense they are opposites.

The *Book of Five Dynasties* tells that Yan Guang was a military official controlling a county. One day he dreamed that a large snake entered his stomach through his belly button. When the snake was almost halfway in, Yan Guang grabbed it and pulled it out. When he awoke, he didn't know what to make of the dream. He was both horrified and fearful of its meaning. He consulted a Daoist monk named Zhang Sheng, who told him that the dream was a good omen because snake belongs to the dragon category, and one who dreams of a dragon entering his stomach will become emperor. Yan Guang became very ambitious, ultimately betraying his emperor, and establishing his own kingdom.

Because it has the nature of Yin, the snake is also considered an animal that is not bright but ghostly, a hunted animal often associated with those who are seductive and not loyal. In the everyday world of the common people, snakes were considered insidious and evil, because they lurked in secret places and could kill with poison bites. Thus some interpreters believe that dreams of snakes portend bad luck. *The New Collection of Zhou Gong's Dream Interpretations* says that "If someone dreams of a snake coming under the bed, it means that the person will have a serious illness. If someone dreams of a snake going up to the roof, it means the coming of a great disaster. If someone dreams of a snake coming into the bed, it means that the person will die. If someone dreams of a snake biting someone, it means his mother will die. If someone dreams of seeing a coiled snake, his house will have trouble. But, if someone dreams of beating a snake, it is great luck." The same text says that if a pregnant woman dreams of a snake it means that she will give birth to a girl.

Yellow Snake

A dream of a yellow snake is a portent of power.

The Grand History tells that when Wen Gong was still a young man and not yet emperor, he went hunting. One night he had a dream that a yellow snake came down from the sky. He asked an interpreter named Shi Dun what this strange dream meant and was told it was a sign of becoming powerful and that sacrifices should be made to make the omen come true. They then offered three cows in sacrifice and Wen Gong soon became emperor.

Spider

A portent of good luck and magical powers.

Since a spider's web is described as being like good silk—fine, strong, gossamer, and so on—the spider that weaves the web is said to be an omen of good luck and a bearer or riches and power. The *Tai Ping Guang Ji* records that a Daoist monk dreamed an old man gave him rolls of silk and said "I am a spider and I am good at weaving. I am dedicating this to you in hopes that you will have land and fine clothes." After saying this, he died. When the monk awoke he found the silk lying next to him; it was indescribably delicate compared to other silks that he had known. He had clothes made of this special silk and found that these amazing garments could not be soiled.

See also Silk

Star

Stars predict the gaining an important special position.

According to *The Family Principles of the Yan,* the ancients considered stars to be the essence of the sky and earth. *On the Principles of Things* states that a dream of stars is like a dream of the sun. Stars relate to the emperor and the relations between his ministers and princes. Interpreters usually considered stars as positive omens, symbols of gaining a special position or status.

The Book of the Northern Dynasty tells that emperor Gao Zu of the northern Qi dreamed that he was walking in the heavens on the stars. He came to believe that this dream was related to his later establishing a kingdom. *The New Tang History* tells that the mother of Li Bai, the famous poet, dreamed about the "star" Chang Geng (Venus), the brightest (whitest) star before giving birth, so she named her son Li Bai (*bai* meaning white). *The Book of Songs* tells that Huang Kang's mother once dreamed that a shooting star fell onto her chest, which she held with her hands. Thereafter she became pregnant and gave birth to Huang Kang, a man who gained great fame during the Song dynasty.

Shooting (Falling) Star
An omen of death.

In contrast to the West, where shooting stars are seen as positive omens, in Chinese dreams they are foreboding omens. *The New Collection of Zhou Gong's Dream Interpretations* states that, "If one dreams of stars it means that he will become an official, but if one dreams of a shooting star there will be trouble in his house." Another text tells that Cai You Xue one day dreamed he saw falling stars that fell to the southwest of his yard. Soon after this ominous dream, he died at age sixty-four. But according to Chen Shi Yuan's book, if one dreams that a star falls upon one's body, it is good luck; however, a dream of a star falling in a wild field means impending evil.

Stomach (see Organs)

Stove

An omen of giving advice or losing one's spouse.
It can also portend a woman in one's family getting married.

Stoves in dreams are seen as devices whereby one can give advice, especially to the emperor. *The Book of Han Fei Zi* records that when Wei Ling Gong was the king of the Wei, he was extremely dictatorial and he relied heavily for advice on a single favorite minister, Mi Zi Xia. A dwarf came to the king and said, "All I dreamed came to be true." Wei Ling Gong asked what he had dreamed that came true, and, the dwarf said, "I dreamed about the stove god and now I see you." The king was enraged, and said, "When people dream of the sun, it is said that they will then see the emperor. You say that before seeing me you dreamed of a stove. How is this?" The dwarf said, "The sun gives light to the universe and nothing can be protected from it. Likewise, the emperor's virtue covers the whole country and no one can resist it; that is why if one dreams of the sun he sees the emperor. But if only one person sits in front of a stove, all the others behind him cannot see the light or feel the heat. At present, when deciding matters of state, you only listen to your favorite, Mi Zi Xia. He is like a person sitting right in front of the stove, blocking the light and heat. Looking at it this way, aren't you more like the stove god than the sun? Therefore, I dreamed of a stove and it is natural that I saw you."

The Chinese characters for "wife" and "cooking in a stone pan" have a similar pronunciation, *fu*. Thus a dream of a stove has been interpreted as an omen of losing one's wife. *The Notes from Youyang* tell the story of a traveling businessman about to return home, who dreamed that he was cooking food in a stone pan. He asked a dream interpreter named Wang Sheng what it meant, and was told, "Although you are returning home, you will not be seeing your wife. Cooking in a stone pan means no *fu*, which is the same as no stove or no wife. The businessman went home to find that his wife had died several months earlier.

Another book on dream interpretation, *Yi Wen Lei Ju,* says that a dream of a stove means that one is thinking about marrying or that a woman in one's family is going to be married.

Sun and Sunlight

A dream of the sun is a dream of royalty.

The early Chinese believed that the sun was the Yang essence of the universe, no doubt related to the reliance the sun for the growth of crops. The sun came to symbolize the emperor, an upright gentleman, sage, or aged person who is to be revered. Chen Shi Yuan records in his Ming dynasty work *Meng Zhan Yi Zhi* that, "The sun and the moon are the symbols of highest nobility." In *The Grand History* it is recorded that emperor Wen Wang of the Zhou dynasty once dreamed that the moon and the sun were attached to his body. *The Book of Han* tells that emperor Wu Di's mother once dreamed that the sun came into her chest. These dreams were regarded as portents of nobility of the highest order.

Early in the Three Kingdoms period Sun Quan's mother dreamed the sun came to her chest. She told this to her husband Sun Jian who felt that this dream was a good omen. She later gave birth to the future emperor. Yet another story tells that when Fan Ying Jin was in his mother's womb, his grandfather dreamed that there were two suns shining in the yard. Fan, after becoming a *jin shi* (passing the imperial level of the civil service examination) was later promoted to a title equivalent to a minister.

Before Mao Zen Fu came to the city of Guangling to accept an official title during the Five Dynasties period, he dreamed that he swallowed the sun. When he awoke, he felt hot and felt heat in his stomach. He asked an interpreter, Yang Ting Shi, what this dream meant and Yang stated that this dream was a portent of great success. Mao was later given a red feather as a sign of office; the red feather supposedly came from a bird that has three feet, and is also regarded as a substitute for the sun. So, Mao's dreaming of the sun was an example of the fortune or good luck.

In a dream recorded *The Spring and Autumn of Yan Zi*, emperor Jing Gong of Qi became ill and stayed in bed for ten days. One day during this illness he dreamed two suns were fighting but could not best one another. A dream interpreter said that the dream foretold Jin Gong's death; he then called Yan Zi, who has a special talent for interpretation. When the dream interpreter tried to find a solution in his books, Yan Zi said, "Let me do it without books." He said, "Your majesty, you have an illness that could be

Yin but the sun belongs to Yang. The two suns fighting without victory means one Yin could not beat two Yangs, meaning you will recover soon and you will be in good health." Three days later, Jin Gong recovered.

Sunlight on a Woman
A pregnancy is in one's immediate future.

Sunlight shining upon the body of a woman in a dream foretells of a pregnancy. An example from the *Book of Ming* tells the story of a writer named Li Meng Yang. Before his mother became pregnant, she had a dream of basking in sunlight. Following this dream, she felt that she was with child and soon after gave birth. She named her son Meng Yang, literally meaning "dreaming the sun."

Documented in *The Book of Yuan* is the story of Yang Huan's mother. Before she gave birth, she dreamed that sunlight was shining from the southeast, covering her entire body. A sage who came and began writing something that she could not see. When she awoke, she told the dream to her father, who reasoned that this was a symbol of literacy and thus gave the baby the name Ri Huan, who indeed became a renowned writer.

Since the sun is the symbol of the emperor, everything that the sun shines upon is therefore is blessed by him. Interpreters believed that a dream of sunlight covering the dreamer's body meant that he or she would be blessed by the emperor and thus be favored and gain great fortune. *The Book of Wei* tells that empress Xiao Wen Zhao once dreamed that she was standing in the hall when sunlight came through the window and covered her body, causing her to feel hot. She tried to avoid the sunlight by moving to other parts of the hall but it continued to cover her. She had this dream several times over the next few days and, feeling that it was strange, she told her father. He consulted the dream interpreter Min Zong ,who interpreted the sunlight as a symbol with an auspicious and noble meaning. He explained that the sun symbolized the virtue of the emperor and the sunlight covering the girl's body meant that she was blessed. So although she tried to avoid the light, it continued to seek her out, something that she could not control. Similar dreams recorded from earlier times indicated that this daughter would be blessed by the favor of the emperor and give birth to a future emperor. Xiao Wen Zhao later gave birth to emperor Shi Zong.

Swallowing

Swallowing Dirt
An omen of death.

Being returned to the earth is synonymous with death and hence a dream of swallowing or eating dirt is associated with death. Emperor Zhi Meng of Liang had a dream in which he saw earth and ate it. Sometime later, his ministers overthrew him and buried him alive. And so, as he dreamed of eating earth, he suffocated at the age of forty-nine in the earth.

Swallowing Flower Petals
A prediction of pregnancy and the birth of a talented child.

Beautiful women are frequently associated with the beauty of flowers, while petals, considered the "fruit" of the flower are associated with children. *Yu Chu Xin Zhi,* a Qing dynasty text by Zhang Chan Lai, tells that the wife of a man named Chan dreamed she swallowed flower petals. After she awoke, she felt that she had become pregnant and indeed she did bear a son nine months later. The son who was born was highly talented and by age nine was able to compose fine poems. He was attracted to plants and flowers and became a very well known scholar of horticulture.

Swallowing Seals
A portent of gaining an official position and social status.

The seal is a symbol of status and authority. Internalizing the seal is a symbol of gaining of status and position, the dream of every civil servant. The book *Qing Xiang Za Ji* tells a story about Liu Zi of the Song dynasty. He dreamed that he swallowed fourteen seals. He then had a series of successes in his taking the civil examinations after the age of forty, and then held fourteen official positions in his life. His dream of swallowing fourteen seals predicted his success.

See also Eating

Sword

Symbols of treasure, respect, or loss of profit or advantage.

Knives and swords are sharp, *li,* pronounced the same as the word for "profit." Therefore, if someone dreamed of sharpening a knife, it meant that profits or riches were coming. But dreams of knives and swords can have other meanings, some of which may seem contradictory. As they are able to kill or wound people, they can be a symbols of losing profit or advantage as well. And because they are weapons used to bring enemies to submission, they can also be symbols of power and respect.

Some interpreters believed that only one respected would appear in a dream with sword in hand; any killing, normally a bad omen, would then be interpreted favorably, as a means of gaining power. A dream of two or more knives striking one another meant that there would be conflict between relatives. A dream of being killed meant that one would gain longevity. A dream of being wounded meant that great fortune would come. One book explains, "Dreaming of injuries and blood portends great fortune. Dreaming of being injured by a knife is an omen of a great life and fortune in one's future."

On the other hand, *The New Collection of Zhou Gong's Dream Interpretations* says that "Dreams of being injured by swords bring losses of to the dreamer; dreams of seeing knife blades bring fortune; dreams of sharpening a knife mean great prosperity and profit; dreams of holding or walking with a knife mean that arguments will be resolved; dreams of giving swords or knives to others cause the dreamer lose profits; dreams of knives hitting each other indicate love affairs; dreams of being killed by a knife give longevity to the dreamer; and dreams of traveling with a sword or knife indicate the nobility of the traveler."

The Book of Jin tells that Wang Jun had a dream in which he saw three knives hanging from the roof beam of the bedroom, and a moment later another knife appeared. When he awoke he was worried that this was an evil omen, but the famed dream interpreter Li Yi congratulated him and said that the dream was a lucky omen. The three knives that had appeared formed the character of *zhou,* meaning "counties" or "regions." The fourth knife then appeared to form the word *yi,* meaning that he would become the governor of the county of Yi. Not long afterward, thieves killed the governor of Yi and Wang Jun was promoted to take his place.

Zhao Zhen Ren, controlling the waves by slaying an evil dragon (Wang).

Tears (see Crying)

Tent

**Refers to the bed tent used in the bedroom,
thus symbolizes the affairs between husband and wife.**

In the early vernacular, if people thought that if someone behaved in a less than virtuous manner, that person was said to be "without a clean tent." Tent dreams are often a symbol of the affairs between male and female.

The Book of Zuo tells of a married woman in Quanzhou who dreamed she saw her bed tent hung in the family temple of Meng Xizi. She ran secretly to Meng and they made love, swearing that even if they had a child they would not betray one another. Later the woman gave birth to two children Meng Yizi, and Jing Shu, and she and her husband gave the second child to the lover to raise.

Thunder

Portends the end of power and the coming of one's death.

Thunder is a sound that comes from the heavens, which, accompanied by a storm, is often frightening and portends ill. *The Dream Book* tells that emperor Zhou of the Shang dynasty had a dream of thunder striking his head. This dream preceded his being overthrown and was felt to have predicted his downfall.

See also Lightning and Thunder

Tiger (see Lion and Tiger)

Tomb

An omen of prosperity.

While tombs and graves are seen by most as places of misfortune, sadness, and death, dream interpreters see them as symbols of good luck. It is said,

"If one sees graves in dreams, it portends great fortune; if one sees trees growing on the tomb, it also portends great fortune; if one sees deep woods growing around the tomb, it means that the whole family will become prosperous; if one dreams of walking on a tomb, it signifies great happiness."

The Book of the Northern Dynasty tells that Yang Xiu Zhi, before taking an office of high rank in Luoyang, had a dream in which he walked into a huge tomb. He climbed up to the top and saw a copper post, the base of which was in the shape of a lotus. He stepped onto the lotus base and held the post, and then started spinning around it, murmuring the curse, "I turn three times around this post and the position for me will be the third rank." He then made three revolutions and stopped. When woke up, Yang remembered the dream and even the direction he faced when he stopped turning, toward the court. He later achieved a position of the third rank at court.

Entering a Tomb with a Torch

**Entering a tomb with a (flaming) torch portends
great fortune or success.**

Tombs of the Chinese were designed to pay homage to ancestors and therefore were places of honor. *The Book of the Northern Qi* records that just before he took his official position, the scholar Li Yuan Zhong dreamed that he entered his father's grave while holding a torch in his hand. He was terrified by this dream and woke up in the middle of the night thinking it was a premonition of ill. He could not get the dream out of his mind, and related it to his teacher. To his surprise, his teacher exclaimed, "What great fortune! This means you have shed light on your ancestors. Riches and high position will definitely be yours."

Tongue

Cutting One's Tongue

A sign of ability speak correctly and with authority.

For those unable to speak correctly because of a speech impediment, life is certainly more difficult. Having a dream of one's tongue being cut is an indication that a correction of the speaking difficulty will come. It is written in the *Shuo Fu* that Wang Fa Lang had such a big tongue it was difficult for him to pronounce words properly. He had a dream that a Daoist god cut his tongue with scissors so that he could speak properly. After his dream, he did indeed begin to speak correctly.

Tree

Trees are symbols of life and prosperity.

Trees are of the nature of Yang and belong to the direction east. As such, they are symbols of life and vitality. The *Analytical Dictionary of Characters* states that "Wood grows from earth and faces east." Interpreters believed that trees in dreams were omens of prosperity. On the other hand, dead trees were seen as omens of ill.

The *New Collection of Zhou Gong's Dream Interpretations* says that, "Dreams of walking in the mountain forests are good omens, as are dreams of seeing forests. Dreams of seeing a tree growing bring good luck to the dreamer; dreams of seeing a tree dying or a dead tree give the dreamer bad luck. Dreams of seeing trees breaking indicate losing a brother; dreams of climbing trees mean that happy events will follow; dreams of seeing trees and grass growing thickly mean that one's household will be prosperous. Dreams of seeing trees dying suddenly mean that one's mother will become ill. Dreams of seeing burning wood in a hall are also unlucky omens."

Specific trees are interpreted differently according to their own symbolic content. The *Tai Ping Yu Lan* says that, "The pine tree is synonymous with heroes, gentlemen, or sages. Therefore dreams of seeing pine trees are signs of seeing emperors or great men." The same book says, "The elm is a symbol of the human virtue of benevolence *(ren)*. Dreams of picking the leaves of the elm portend being favored by the emperor. Dreams of living in an elm will bring the dreamer a high-ranking official position, while dreams of elms with abundant branches and leaves means increased happiness and wealth." It further states, "The willow tree is a symbol of a messenger. Dreams of seeing a willow tree indicate traveling away from the home."

See also Pine, Willow

Turtle

The turtle is an omen of good luck and longevity.

The turtle was known as the favored of those animals with a shell, a symbol of longevity and therefore a lucky omen in a dream. The *Book of Spring and Autumn of the Ten Countries* tells that when Liu Zan was young, he was not clever. His writing lacked imagination and showed his ignorance. He prayed daily to be blessed with literary talents but to no avail, until one day he dreamed of a golden turtle. From then his articles and essays improved greatly and he was promoted to a provincial level official. He subsequently dreamed again of a golden turtle but in this dream he spit it out. Soon after he died.

Chen Shi Yuan's book tells of an official named Sheng Yu, who dreamed a Daoist monk gave him a golden turtle. Sheng Yu wrote a poem in honor of the turtle that said, "In the dream I saw people coming with a baby boy, and then I was given a golden turtle. If tomorrow my wife gives birth to a child, it will be a boy with a handsome face." Soon afterward his wife bore him a son.

By contrast, *The New Collection of Zhou Gong's Dream Interpretations* says that if someone dreams of seeing a turtle, it means that there will be quarreling, while if someone dreams of a large tortoise, everything will be work out fine.

Voices (from the Dead)

Express the wishes of the dead.

Early texts identified two souls in the human body, *hun* and *po*. *Po* is said to be at one with the body while *hun* is flexible and is at one with the spirits. After death *po* is said to disappear but *hun* continues its existence by leaving the body and rising to the sky as a spirit. Therefore when a person dies, his *hun* soul could visit other relatives and communicate with them by entering their dreams.

The Collection of Literary Essays tells of close friends Fan Shi and Zhang Yuan Bo. Fan, who held a position as deputy county governor dreamed one night of his friend Zhang, who came running to him, wearing a black hat and shouting, "I am dead. Please come to the funeral to participate in the

Huang An, a god of longevity, on the back of turtle, a symbol of longevity (Wang).

rituals, so we will never forget each other." Fan awoke to find that his friend had indeed died, and went to his funeral to participate in the rituals.

The Book of Wei says Lu Yuan Ming, who lived in the east of Luoyang, was a very good friend of Wang You. One evening Lu dreamed that Wang was offered him wine and bid him goodbye. In the dream they wrote several poems to each other, as was the custom of good friends parting. When he awoke, Lu remembered ten words from the poem in the dream, which said, "Since I am leaving now, we can no longer enjoy being together." Lu felt that something strange was happening, and three days later learned that his good friend had been killed in an uprising on the very night of his dream.

Wall (see Pavilion)

Water

Clear, precious water is an auspicious symbol.

Water was pronounced the blood or the essence of both sky and earth, the nourisher of all things and controlled by the gods in heaven, obviously related to the fact that water was so necessary for raising crops. *The Book of Guan Zi* states that water is the "blood" of the earth, just as blood traverses the body through blood vessels. Interpreters considered water dreams as portents of luck. *The New Collection of Zhou Gong's Dream Interpretations* states that "If one dreams of one being in the water, it is great fortune; if one dreams of drinking water, he will receive money and clothes. But dreaming of the river or ocean waves is a grave omen and dreaming that there is no water or of a drought is an evil omen."

The Remaining Books of Dunhuang says, "If one dreams that there is no more water or water is running out, it means that additional misfortunes are coming. Dreams of clean water are fortunate, while dirty water portends evil." This same book explains that water is an extreme Yin object. If Yin comes to an end or is too strong, it will then connect with Yang air. Yin and Yang connecting indicates a liaison between men and women, perhaps marriage and intercourse. Therefore dreaming of floods or great water was interpreted as foretelling marriage.

Water is also associated with the position of Si Kou, a title for the official in charge of criminal sentences, as recorded in *The Rites of Zhou*. Another text also says that water is synonymous with the position of Si Kou and that "Those who carry out the laws are like water." Most dream interpreters believed that a dream of running water meant that the dreamer would become an official, while *The New Collection of Zhou Gong's Dream Interpretations* says that "If one dreams of running water there will be a lawsuit."

The History of the Three Kingdoms tells that Deng Ai had a dream before the war with the kingdom of Shu. In the dream he was sitting on top of a mountain with water running down from it. He asked an interpreter about the meaning of this dream and was told that according to the *Book of Change*, water on top of a mountain was a positive omen for the southwest but not fortunate for the northwest. Even Confucius in his commentary on the *Book of Change* mentioned the southwest in a dream would indicate success and victory while the northeast indicated unfavorable results. Deng Ai was told "Because the Shu Kingdom is in the southwest, if you go in that direction, there will be victory; however, you should not go to the northeast. History proved this interpretation true.

The Jade Sea tells of a Song emperor who became ill and dreamed that the Yellow River was drying up. He became quite worried since the symbol of the emperor is the dragon, thought to bring beneficial rain; if the river dried up, the dragon would have no place to live. He presumed these images meant that death was coming. The interpreter, however, through analyzing characters, explained that word meaning "a river without water" sounds like the character for *ke* (meaning "yes," or "can be") meaning that the emperor's illness could be treated and recovery would come. Soon the emperor did indeed recover.

See also Dragon

Water God

Dreaming of the water god symbolizes filial piety.

The Jin dynasty text *Shui Jing Zhu*, one of the earliest and most important books on geography, tells of Bo Qi, a most devoted son who honored his parents. After his mother died he wore clothes of seaweed as a sign of his filial piety. One day he dreamed of the water god, who gave him medicine to help him become he missed his parents so. He suddenly began to sing sad songs, and the boatmen on the nearby river heard his songs and sang along. Under the water, his parents heard the boatman's songs and thought it was their son. Because of this story, sad songs made or sung after seeing the water god in a dream are associated with devotion to one's parents.

Weapon

See Bow and Arrow, Knife, Sword

Well

A symbol of virtue and possible riches.

The well is the container or source of water, a Yin element that possesses the nature of cleanliness and tranquility. It sustains the life of the common people, and is considered an inexhaustible and dependable resource, a symbol of virtue, and, on a more mundane level, a place where people are able to live. In Chinese, the expression *shi jing* or *jing shi,* means "public well," and refers to a marketplace. The availability of water determined where a public market could be located, and thus wells and well water came to symbolize connectedness, not only for sustenance but also for information.

Water sources are also symbols of fortune, so a well or well water in a dream portends prosperity for the dreamer. Another interpretation, however, holds that since the shape of the well is narrow and deep, it can it indicate being imprisoned or close-minded; the latter is illustrated by such expressions as "like a frog at the bottom of a well" and "looking at the sky while being at the bottom of a well," both describing a limited viewpoint and unfortunate circumstances. *The New Collection of Zhou Gong's Dream Interpretations* offers both good and bad interpretations: "If one dreams that he is going into a well and out again, it means that he will become extremely rich; if one dreams of merely seeing a well, it means that he will soon gain information; but if one dreams of lying in a well, it is a bad omen."

Wheel

**A dream of the wheels of a horse cart is a prediction
of problems between husband and wife.**

Conflicts in the relationship between the husband and wife are seen if one
dreams of wheels of a cart. *The Copied Books in Bei Tang Studio* states that,
"The wheels and the axle are signs of husband and wife. If one dreams of
wheels and the axle, it indicates that either the husband or wife is having an
affair." This is an indication that there is a problem in the relationship,
which will surely lead to further difficulties.

See also Cart

Willow

A portent of going away from one's home.

Willow trees in dreams have been interpreted with with respect to homophones, words that have the same pronunciation but different meanings.
There is a story about Liu Zong Yuan of the Tang dynasty, a great man of
letters who one day dreamed of a willow tree (*liu*) falling down. He worried
and fretted over this dream as his family name was also Liu, the same as the
willow tree, and then he sought out an interpreter, who told him not to
worry. "*Liu* also means parting," he said, "So you should be thinking about
being posted to a far away place."

Wind

Portends selection of a supportive and loyal subordinate.

This is one of several types of dreams that relate to choosing loyal ministers.
The Grand History tells that Huang Di, the Yellow Emperor, once dreamed
of a strong wind that blew away all the dust under heaven while also seeing
someone holding a heavy bow and arrow and driving thousands of sheep.
After he awoke, he surmised that, "The wind (*feng*) means the order of

heaven, a symbol of control, while dust *(chen)* is a character made up of 'dirt' *(tu)* and 'after' *(hou)*." Thinking that the huge bow was a symbol of unusual strength while the ten thousand sheep referred to a great shepherd, he believed that dream was telling him to search for a person having the family name "wind" *(feng)* and personal name "after" *(hou)*. He further wondered if there was a person named "strength" *(li)* and person named "shepherding" *(mu)*, and sent orders to find people who had the names Feng Hou and Li Mu. Finally a person named Feng Hou was located, and given the position of prime minister, while a Li Mu was found and made a general. Both men turned out to be honest and capable, while the Yellow Emperor later wrote *The Book of Interpreting Dreams* in eleven volumes.

The Book of Shang states that during the Shang dynasty, emperor Gao Zong dreamed that the Heavenly Emperor sent him a prime minister to help him run the country. Gao Zong drew a picture of the man in his dream and asked his ministers to look everywhere for him. Finally they found someone with similar features. Although he was only a humble laborer, he was given the position anyway, and became an excellent prime minster.

The Book of Zhuang Zi says that when emperor Wen Wang of the Zhou dynasty was on pleasure excursion, he met a Daoist scholar and wanted to ask him to serve as prime minister. However he was afraid that his other ministers and his brothers would not approve or obey him. They next morning, he assembled all of his ministers and told them that he had dreamed his father told him that he must ask a Daoist believer to be the prime minister. This Daoist official would save the country and improve the lives of the people. All the ministers accepted this dream portent and welcomed the Daoist monk, who indeed turned out to be an excellent prime minister. Confucius commented that this type of dream was usually suited to the needs of the times.

Wine

A sign of welcoming or seeing friends off on a journey.

As in the rest of the world, wine in China is something to be enjoyed and shared between friends and acquaintances. Dreaming of wine portends welcoming friends or seeing them safely off on a journey. The *Bei Tang Shu Chao* says that a dream of wine or liquor means getting ready to welcome friends or see them off on a journey.

Kong Yuan, drinking wine while upside-down and holding a cane (Wang).

Wolf

An omen of unsuccessful travel.

The wolf is a wild beast unfriendly to all. The *Book of Jin* records that Zhang Miao once dreamed of a wolf biting his foot. The well-known interpreter Suo Chen said that it was a sign to avoid travel. Zhang decided not leave for his planned trip and later learned that others who continued on with the trip despite this warning met with disaster.

Worm

Symbolizes a person of strength and reliance.

Records of Strange Stories in Luoyang states that just before he invaded the capital at Chang An (today's Xi'an), the first emperor of the Tang dynasty, Li Yuan, dreamed that he was in bed sleeping but then fell to the floor and died. He saw worms and insects eating his whole body. Li Yuan was greatly disturbed by this dream, assuming it portended bad luck, and secretly revealed it to a Buddhist priest. When he had finished, the priest immediately arose and congratulated him. Kowtowing to him the priest said, "This is a dream of great fortune." He then explained, "Death is the end of all, and is therefore called *bi,* meaning "end," while falling downward is *xia.* The words *bi xia,* however, have the same sound as the words for 'Your Majesty, the emperor.' The insects or worms represent all life; their eating your body means that millions of ordinary people will come to rely on you for food and life itself." When Li Yuan heard this, he became ecstatic. When he later became emperor, he constructed a temple, in which was a hall called Yuan Meng Tang, meaning Dream Realizing Hall. Inside was placed statues of the emperor and the Buddhist priest.

SOURCES AND BIBLIOGRAPHY

The dream interpretations in this book are drawn from numerous original Chinese sources, including standard dynastic histories, anthologies, philosophical texts, and imperial compilations. The titles listed below are more unusual or relate more specifically to dream interpretation.

Bei Ji Qian Jin Yao Fang (Key Precious Prescriptions for Emergencies). Sun Si Miao, Tang dynasty. Gives explanations of dreams based on medical principles.

Bei Tang Shu Chao (The Copied Books in Bei Tang). Edited by Yu Shi Nan, Tang dynasty. A compilation of excerpts from various books, in 160 volumes covering 852 subjects. (*Bei tang* refers to the "rear hall" of the ministry of education.)

Chao Ye Qian Zai (A Complete Collection of Court and Popular Stories). Compiled by Zhang Zhuo, Tang dynasty. Anecdotes from the Jin and Tang dynasties, originally in 6 volumes, but the original book is lost.

Du Yi Zhi (Records of the Unique and the Strange). Compiled by Li Rong, Tang dynasty. Stories and anecdotes, mostly from other books, in 10 volumes.

Er Cheng Ji (The Collection of the Cheng Brothers). Cheng Yi, Song dynasty. The ideas of the brothers Cheng Ying and Cheng Yi strongly influenced Confucianism and thus Chinese history. This work, based on the story of Confucius dreaming of seeing Zhou Gong, gives the Confucian perspective on dream interpretation.

Fa Yuan Zhu Lin (The Legal Garden and Pearl Forest). Compiled by Dao Shi, Tang dynasty. Buddhist stories and ancient myths and legends in 100 volumes (there are also popular versions in 120 volumes).

Gu Jin Ying Meng Yi Meng Quan Shu (A Complete Collection of the Coming-true Dreams and Strange Dreams in Ancient Times and Today). Zhang Gan Shan, Ming dynasty. A collection of stories related to dreams, in 4 volumes.

Guan Zi (The Book of Guan Zi). Purportedly by Guan Zhong of the Three Kingdoms period, but in fact, a later compilation. A philosophical work, but also with many myths, originally in 86 chapters, 10 now lost.

Han Fei Zi (The Book of Han Fei Zi). Purportedly by Han Fei of the Warring States period, but in fact a later collection of his works. Presents the Legalist thought of the period, but includes many myths and legends, 55 chapters in 20 volumes.

Han Fu Ming Tan (Famous Talks in the Han Mansion).

Han Yu Wen Ji (Collection of Han Yu's Works). Han Yu.

Hang Zhi (Ethnography of Hangzhou).

He Tu Di Tong Ji (A General Record of the Emperor He Tu).

Hong Fan Wu Xing Zhuan (The Records of Hong Fan's Studies on the Five Elements).

Hou Han Shu (The Book of the Later Han). Fan Ye, Southern dynasty. A history, but containing many folk tales and myths, in 120 volumes.

Hua Yang Guo Zhi (Ethnography of Huayang). Chang Qu, Jin dynasty. The history of Bashu (the area of present-day Sichuan) from its origins to the year of 347, containing many myths and legends among historical facts, in 12 volumes.

Huai Nan Zi (The Prince of Huai Nan). Compiled by Prince Liu An and his fellow scholar guests during the Han dynasty. A compendium of philosophical thought, mostly of Daoist, also called the *Huai Nan Hong Lie.* Only 21 volumes remain of the original 54.

Huan Tan Xin Lun (The New Views of Huan Tan).

Huang Di Nei Jing (The Yellow Emperor's Book of Internal Medicine).

Hui Ji Xian Xian Zhuan (A Biography of the Early Sages in Hui Ji).

Ji Meng Yao Lan (A Glimpse of Dreams). Tong Xuan, Ming dynasty. A collection of dreams and theories about interpreting dreams, by a minister of the justice in the imperial court, in 6 volumes by. The original work is lost, but there are excerpts from this book in later compilations.

Ji Shen Lu (Records of the Gods in Ji). Xu Xuan, Southern Tang dynasty.

Ji Yi Ji (A Collection of Strange Stories). Xue Yong Ruo, Tang dynasty.

Ji Yi Lu (A Collection of the Unusual).

Jian Wen Lu (A Collection of Things Seen and Heard).

Jie Jia Xian Ren Zhan Meng Shu (Dream Book of the Monk from Jiejia). Purportedly written by an Indian monk who came to China during the Eastern Han period. A single volume on Buddhist interpretation of dreams, now lost, but included the Sui dynastic history and later compilations.

Jun Ge Ya Tan (Elegant Talks in the Studio Jun Ge).

Kai Yuan Tian Bao Yi Shi Ji (Strange Stories in the Years of Kai Yuan Tian Bao).

Kai Yuan Yi Shi (Stories Passed Down from Kai Yuan Era).

Kuo Yi Zhi (The Enlarged Collection of Strange Stories).

Lao Xue An Bi Ji (Notes from the Studio Lao Xue An). Lu You, Song dynasty.

Liao Zhai Zhi Yi (A Collection of Strange and Ghost Stories). Pu Song Ling, Qing dynasty. A collection of 491 short ghost stories, reflecting the lives of the common people and their beliefs and customs.

Lie Zi (The Book of Lie Zi). Lie Yu Kou of the Warring States period, although the existing edition is believed to date from Jin dynasty. Contains numerous many myths and folk stories, in 8 volumes.

Ling Ying Zhuan (A Biography of Ling Ying). Anonymous, Tang dynasty.

Lun Heng (On Eternity). Wang Chong, Eastern Han dynasty. An important ancient work by the first influential atheist in Chinese history, whose materialist philosophy exerted great influence on later generations, 85 chapters in 30 volumes.

Luo Yang Jia Lan Ji (A Record of Buddhist Temples in Luoyang). Yang Xuanzhi, Northern

Wei (Southern and Northern Dynasties). A Buddhist work including realistic records of the social changes in the author's time, in 5 volumes.

Luo Zhong Ji Yi Lu (Records of the Strange Stories in Luoyang).

Meng Jun (Outstanding Dreams). Edited by Liu Can, Tang dynasty. Although the original version is lost, many of the stories were collected or quoted in such later collections as *Tai Ping Guang Ji* and *Meng Zhan Yi Zhi.*

Meng Lin Yuan Jie (Complete Interpretation of Dreams). Chen Shi Yuan, Ming dynasty, and re-edited by He Dong Ru, also in the Ming dynasty. A key text in Chinese dream interpretation, summarizing previous works and giving systematic interpretations, in 34 volumes.

Meng Shu (The Book of the Dream). Lu Zhong Xuan, Tang dynasty. Lu was a Daoist master and thus his work is representative of Daoist interpretation of dreams, in 4 volumes. Though the original text is lost, it is included in later compilations.

Meng Zhan Lei Kao (An Investigation into Dream Interpretations). Zhang Feng Yi, Ming dynasty. A collection of dreams mentioned in the early classics, each with commentary and assigned to one of 34 categories, in 12 volumes. Although the original version is lost, it is recorded in the standard Ming history.

Meng Zhan Yi Zhi (The Leisure and Pleasure of Interpreting Dreams). Chen Shi Yuan, Ming dynasty. An important book on dreams by a great Confucian scholar whose theoretical framework of dream interpretation is still well known, in 8 volumes.

Ming Yin Lu (Record of the Sounds of the Other World). Anonymous, Tang dynasty.

Nanke Taishou Zhuan (A Biography of Governor Nanke). Li Gong Zuo, Tang dynasty.

Pi Po Sha Lun (The Book of Pi Po Sha). Translated by Xuan Zang, Tang dynasty.

Qian Ding Lu (Records of Predestined Fortune). Zhong Luo, Tang dynasty.

Qian Fu Lun (On Human Potentials). Wang Fu, Eastern Han dynasty. An important book on dream-interpreting theory, classifying dreams into ten types, with systematic explanations.

Qian Shu (The Book of Potentials). Li Liang, Song dynasty.

Qin Meng Ji (Records of the Dreams of Qin). Shen Yazhi, Tang dynasty.

Qing Bo Za Zhi (Random Notes by Qing Bo).

Qing Xiang Za Ji (Random Notes of the Qing Xiang Studio).

San Meng Ji (Records of Three Dreams). Bai Xingjian, Tang dynasty.

Shan Hai Jing (The Book of Mountains and Seas). Regarded as the work of multiple authors the late Warring States period and early Han dynasty. An ancient text containing many earliest myths, in 18 chapters.

Shang Shu (The Book of Shang). Purportedly edited by Confucius, one of the oldest books of Chinese history, presenting myth and historical fact intertwined.

Shao Shi Jian Wen Lu (Records of Shao's Travels).

Shen Si Ying Meng Lu (The True Happenings of the Dreams Interpreted by Gods).

Shi Jing (The Book of Songs). Purportedly edited by Confucius, completed in the Spring and Autumn period. The earliest collection of Chinese poetry, containing 305 songs, or poems, of three genres, believed to be realistically descriptive of the culture and society in which they circulated.

Shi Yi Ji (A Book of Remaining Stories). Compiled by Wang Jia, Jin dynasty, and further supplemented by Liang Xiao Yi, Southern dynasty. Numerous myths and legends, in 10 volumes.

Shu Ju Zi (Shu Ju Zi). Zhuang Yuan Chen, Ming dynasty. Mainly Buddhist interpretations of dreams, emphasizing the function of "heart" in thinking and knowing, and in dreaming.

Shuo Wen Jie Zi (Analytical Dictionary of Characters). Originally edited by Xu Chen, Han dynasty, in 15 volumes, and re-edited by Xu Xuan, Song dynasty in 30 volumes. The earliest dictionary of Chinese characters, and thus a key reference in Chinese language and culture.

Song Shi (A Collection of Song [dynasty] Poems).

Sou Shen Hou Ji (A Supplement to a Collection of Spirits). Purportedly edited by Tao Qian, but in fact collected by editors in the Southern and Northern Dynasties.

Sou Shen Ji (A Collection of Spirits). Gan Bao, Jin dynasty. Ghost stories, myths, and legends, in 20 volumes, a key source for Chinese folklore studies.

Sui Tang Jia Hua (Anecdotes of the Sui and Tang Dynasties).

Tan Cong (Talking Bushes).

Tan Yuan (Speech Garden).

Tian Shan Yu Nu Ji (Stories of the Jade Girl on Mount Tianshan). Jia Shan Xiang, Jin dynasty.

Wang Sheng (Biography of Wang Sheng). Cheng Zhixiang, Qing dynasty.

Wen Xin Diao Long (The Literary Heart and the Carving of Dragons). Liu Xie, Southern and Northern dynasties. The earliest work on literary theory, containing 25 chapters in two parts.

Wu He Ji (A Collection of the Senseless). Xiong Bo Long, Qing dynasty. A practical guide for using dream interpretation for political and religious purposes.

Xi Jing Za Ji (A Sketch of Xijing). Liu Yin, Han dynasty, perhaps a pseudonym of Ge Hong, Jin dynasty. Anecdotes and folk tales from the period of Emperor Wu Di of the Han dynasty, in 6 volumes.

Xie Xiao E Zhuan (Biography of Xie Xiao E). Li Gong Zuo, Tang dynasty.

Xin Ji Zhou Gong Jie Meng Shu (The New Collection of Zhou Gong's Dream Interpretations). Unknown author, Tang dynasty. Covers various dream symbolism and interpretation in 23 chapters. Supposedly based on the original *Zhou Gong Jie Meng Shu (Zhou Gong's Dream Interpretations)* in 3 volumes, lost, except for a few fragments, even in early times. It may be that neither text is actually connected to Zhou Gong, which refers to Emperor Ji Dan of the early Zhou dynasty.

Xun Zi (The Book of Xun Zi). Xun Zi (Xun Kuang), Warring States Period. A philosophical work, but containing many myths, in 20 volumes.

Yan Shi Jia Xun (Yan Family Principles). Yan Zhi Tui, Southern and Northern dynasties. As a way to present rules of conduct for his children, the author includes various stories to illustrate Confucian virtues, in 20 chapters.

Yan Zi Chun Qiu (The Spring and Autumn of Yan Zi). A collection of historical essays about Yan Zi, a statesman of Qi during the Spring and Autumn Period, in 250 chapters.

Yao Di Pao Zhuang (The Village of Medicine and Weapons). Fang Yi Zhi, Ming dynasty. Fang theorized that dreams were the reflections in sleep of the thinking of the mind in an awakened state.

Yi Jian Zhi (The Stories of the Foreign). Compiled by Hong Mai, Song dynasty. A compendium of mostly myths and folk tales, with 200 volumes remaining of the original 420 volumes.

Yi Jing or *Zhou Yi (The Book of Change)*. Purportedly edited by Confucius. The central text of Chinese philosophy, myth, and folk belief, introducing the 64 hexagrams and their 384 variations believed to explain the operation of Yin and Yang throughout all existence.

Yi Meng Lu (Records of Strange Dreams). Shen Yazhi, Tang dynasty.

Yi Wen Lei Ju (Collection of Literary Essays). Ouyang Xun, et. al, Tang dynasty. A compilation of references to more than one thousand books, few of which exist today, in 48 categories totalling 100 volumes.

Yi Yuan (A Garden of the Unusual). Liu Jing Shu, Southern dynasty. Myths and ghost stories, in 10 volumes.

Yin Hua Lu (Records of Casual Conversations).

Ying Meng Lu (Records of True Happenings). Zhan Xing Yuan. The original text is lost, although parts exists in later compilations.

Ying Tao Qing Yi (Cherry and Black Clothes). Anonymous, Tang dynasty.

You Ming Lu (Records of the Dark and the Bright). Compiled by Liu Yiqing, Southern dynasty. Mostly myths and ghost stories in 30 volumes (other sources say 20 volumes) now lost but referred to in other compilations

You Yang Za Zu (Notes from Youyang). Compiled by Duan Cheng Shi, Tang dynasty. Myths, anecdotes, folk tales, and ghost stories (many included in this book), in 30 volumes.

Yu Hai (The Jade Sea).

Yue Jue Shu (The Book of the Extremes). Compiled by Yuan Kang, Han dynasty. Mostly folk tales and myths, originally in 25 volumes, with only 15 extant.

Yun Ji Qi Jian (Book of Clouds and Seven Divining Sticks). Zhang Jun Fang, Song dynasty. Myths and anecdotes primarily from the Daoist tradition, in 122 volumes.

Yun Xian Za Ji (Random Notes on the Cloud Immortals).

Zhan Meng Shu (The Book of Dreams). Zhou Xuan, et. al, Three Kingdoms period. An important work by a noted dream interpreter. Although the original version is lost, parts of the text appear in standard histories of the Sui and Song.

Zhang Meng Shu (The Book of Dreams). Compiled by Jing Fang, Western Han dynasty. Illustrative of Confucian interpretation of dreams, by an important Confucian and well-known literary critic. The original text in 3 volumes is lost, but appears in later compilations.

Zhang Meng Shu (The Book of Dreams). Wang Sheng. Although the original version in 10 volumes is lost, parts of the text appear in standard histories of the Sui and Song.

Zhang Zai Ji (The Collection of Zhang Zai). Zhang Zai, Northern Song dynasty. Proposes a theory that "heart feeling" (xin gan) is the cause of *Zhen Zhong Ji (Stories on Pillow)*. Li Bi, Tang dynasty.

Zheng Meng (On Enlightenment). Zhang Zai, Song dynasty.

Zhou Li (The Rites of Zhou). The title refers to the rituals of rulers of the Zhou dynasty (1100–256 BC). Although the original text is no longer extant, later texts contain many references this work, which contains the earliest references to dreams and proposes a "three-dream" classification system (see "Theories and Dream Interpreters").

Zhuang Zi (The Book of Zhuang Zi). Zhuang Zhou, et. al, Warring States period. A book of myth, metaphysical speculation, and philosophy by a Daoist folk hero who had great impact on Chinese thought and culture. Of the 52 chapters in the original version, only 33 remain, with 7 believed to be the work of Zhuang Zi, the rest by his students.

The "weathermark" identifies this book as a production of Weatherhill, Inc., publishers of fine books on Asia and the Pacific. Editorial supervision: Ray Furse. Book and cover design: Mariana Canelo. Production supervision: Bill Rose. Printing and binding: R.R. Donnelley & Co. The typefaces used are Garamond and Snell Roundhand.